Martinique

2025

Shelly Wharton

Copyright Disclaimer

This disclaimer states that all material in the book, such as text, images, and illustrations, is copyrighted. While the author and publisher have taken steps to ensure accuracy, they make no guarantees about the reliability of the information. Readers should use their own judgment when using the content, and the author and publisher are not responsible for any damages that may occur.

Reproduction or distribution of the content without prior written permission is strictly prohibited, and references to external sources are provided for informational purposes only. This disclaimer protects the author's rights and informs readers of their responsibilities regarding the book's content.

© 2024 Shelly Wharton. All rights reserved.

- Activities
- Beach
- Nightlife/Bars
- Hotels/Accommodations
- Restaurants
- Hike Spot
- Museum/Historical Landmark
- Tourist site/attraction

Note
The number of dollar signs ($, $$, $$$, $$$$) indicates the average cost per person for a meal at the restaurant, with more dollar signs representing higher prices.

Please note that prices, including entry fees for tourist sites, are subject to change from the date this guide was created.

Here's a guide on making the most of the QR code maps featured in this guidebook:

Step 1: Prepare your device by ensuring your smartphone or tablet has a camera and internet connection.

Step 2: Open your camera app. You don't need to take a picture; your camera acts as a QR code scanner.

Step 3: Focus on the QR code in your guidebook, aligning it within your camera's view.

Step 4: Scan the QR code. Your device will automatically recognize it, and a notification or pop-up will appear. Tap to open the link.

Step 5: You'll be directed to an interactive map or webpage with detailed instructions for the location in the guidebook.

Step 6: Explore the map to discover the area, get directions, find points of interest, and effectively use the guidebook's instructions.

Step 7: Make sure you have an internet connection, preferably mobile data or Wi-Fi, to load the map and access real-time information.

Step 8: Keep in mind that maps may change over time. If you return to the map later, ensure your guidebook is updated with the latest QR code.

Using a QR code map in your guidebook enhances your exploration experience by offering interactive and dynamic guidance to enrich your travels or adventures.

Interesting Facts About Martinique

Did you know....?

CORAL PARADISE.
The Martinique reefs explode with color – home to over 50 species of coral, from delicate soft varieties to vibrant hard corals. Beautiful for ocean adventurers.

BREATHTAKING SCENE
Stunning landscapes, with vibrant green slopes, the majestic Mount Pelée volcano, and lush tropical forests interspersed with banana plantations – a captivating sight during any journey across the island.

THE ISLAND IS CLEAN
Martinique stands out for its exceptional cleanliness. The streets and beaches are well-kept, reflecting the locals' respect and care for their environment, making it a refreshing retreat.

Turtle Sanctuary
Endangered sea turtles, like the majestic hawksbill and leatherback, find a safe haven to nest and breed within the reefs of Martinique

Mouthwatering Cuisines.
Martinique offers delicious fusion of French, African, and Creole cuisine! creating a unique dining experience. From fresh, colorful fruits and spices for vegans to delectable seafood dishes like accra and dorade grilée, there's something to tantalize every palate.

Contents

Overview of Martinique 14

  History and Culture 14

  Landscape and Climate 16

  Seasons and Best Time to Visit Martinique 16

Planning Your Trip 18

  Getting there 18

  Getting Around 20

The Guide - Martinique 22

  Fort de France 22

    Getting There 23

    Getting Around 23

    Tourist Attractions 24

    Culinary 40

    Where to Stay 43

    Itinerary 45

  Sainte Anne 48

    Getting There 51

    Getting Around 51

    Tourist attractions 51

    Culinary – Where to Eat 65

    Accommodation – Where to Stay 67

    Itinerary 69

  Saint-Pierre 74

    Getting There 75

    Navigating Around Sainte Pierre 76

    Tourist Attraction 76

Accommodation – Where to Stay 88

Where to Eat – Restaurants 89

Itinerary 92

Trois-Ilets 94

Getting there 95

Navigating Around Trois Ilet 95

Tourist Attraction 96

Accommodations – where to stay 105

Itinerary 106

Le Francois 108

Getting There 108

How to Get Around 108

Tourist Attractions 110

Accommodations – where to stay 118

Le Diamant 121

Getting There 121

Getting Around 121

Tourist Attractions 122

Other Noteworthy Areas to Visit in Martinique 131

Tourist Attractions 131

Spas 163

Itineraries 166

Practical information 168

Health Info and COVID Regulations 168

Safety 168

Travel With Children 169

Travel With Pets 169

Communication and Emergency Contacts 169

Money Matters 170

Language and local life 170

Martinique Month-by-Month: Festivals & Fun 171

Maps 178

Martinique 178

Fort de France 179

Sainte Anne 180

Sainte Pierre 181

Trois Ilet 182

Le Francois 183

Le Diamant 184

Why Visit Martinique - A Captivating Blend of Nature, Culture, and Adventure

I had heard good things about Martinique, but I was still amazed by how vibrant and lively it was. As soon as I stepped off the airplane, I was surrounded by lush greenery, a warm welcome from the island. The steep hillsides were densely covered with vegetation, interrupted only by the imposing shadow of Mount Pelée. Though no longer active, the volcano still serves as a powerful reminder of the island's geological roots.

Exploring Martinique felt like an adventure. The winding roads took me through endless banana plantations, revealing stunning beaches and the Caribbean Sea in shades of blue that seemed almost unreal. But sunbathing isn't the only activity here; the island invites you to immerse yourself in its natural wonders.

The unique blend of European and Caribbean influences is evident everywhere. My days began with fresh croissants from a local boulangerie and ended at bustling markets where vendors sold homegrown produce. The vibrant mix of spices and the vivid colors of mangoes, avocados, and other exotic fruits created an unforgettable sensory experience. Martinique's cleanliness is striking—there is no litter, even in urban areas, reflecting the locals' respect for their environment. Food lovers will be delighted by Martinique's culinary diversity. The island offers spicy Creole seafood dishes and delicious vegetarian options made from local produce, catering to every palate.

Discovering that Martinique is home to some of the world's best snorkeling spots, I couldn't wait to dive in. The crystal-clear waters revealed colorful fish and even a few turtles. For those seeking more excitement, the island offers surfing, kitesurfing, and hiking up waterfalls—sure to get anyone's adrenaline pumping.

Martinique leaves a lasting impression. Visitors return time and again, enchanted by its breathtaking landscapes, rich culture, and delicious cuisine. Once you've experienced this Caribbean paradise, you'll find yourself longing to return again and again.

~ From the Author

Overview of Martinique

Located in the southeast Caribbean Sea, Martinique lies between Dominica to the north and Saint Lucia to the south. An overseas department of France, Martinique shows traces of both French and Caribbean culture, but most especially through its cuisine, which is a delicious mix of French and Creole flavors. It measures about 436 square miles (1,128 square km) of area, making Martinique one of the most densely populated islands in the Antilles. The landscape of the island is rather varied: one would find black-sand beaches and dense forests in the northern part of the island, while very famous, tourist-friendly, wonderful beaches are found in the south. It is topped by Mount Pelée, at 4,583 feet. This famous volcano erupted on May 8, 1902, destroying the city of Saint Pierre and killing thirty thousand people.

History and Culture

Nestled in the sea of the southeast Caribbean, Martinique offers a vibrant mix of French and Caribbean influences that create a most unique cultural experience. Being a French overseas department, it skillfully merges traditions from both worlds—a trait highly and delightfully expressed through its cuisine. Just imagine dishes entwining the sophistication of French culinary techniques with bold flavors characteristic of Creole. Martinique is a very historic and culturally complex island that has faced many pivotal events and cultural shifts. Christopher Columbus first encountered the island on January 15, 1502. Due to its snake infestation, Columbus remained on the island only for three days because it was quite hostile to him. He named it after the indigenous people and called it Matino or Madinina, which is "the island of women" or "the island of flowers." Prior to Columbus' coming, two tribes, the Arawaks and the Caribs, were inhabiting the island. The Arawaks were gentle people who migrated from Central America, while the Caribs were fierce warriors from the Venezuelan coast who came at the turn of the 11th century. By the time Columbus arrived, the Caribs had overrun the Arawaks, keeping their women for domestic use.

It wasn't until 1632 that Martinique was really affected when the French explorer Pierre Belain d'Esnambuc landed on the island. He settled in what is now Saint-Pierre, and his nephew, Du Parquet, was the first governor of the island. Initial agreements were made between him and the Caribs, but soon the war erupted and the Caribs were pushed towards the cliffs, whereby legend has it many went over. In this period, the island saw unprecedented economic development through large plantations of tobacco, indigo, cotton, and, above all, sugar cane. Most of these industries required human power, and thus, there was an importation of African slaves during this period between 1686 and 1720. This also formed a period of rivalry amongst the European powers; in 1674, the island was briefly occupied by the Dutch. Martinique did not experience the direct impact of the 1789 French Revolution and took refuge under British protection to avoid revolutionary violence. The British occupied the island in 1804 but pulled out in 1814. A native of Martinique, Marie Josèphe Rose, married Napoleon Bonaparte and became Empress Josephine in 1804. Under influences from Josephine, Napoleon briefly restored slavery in 1802, but enslavement was finally and completely abolished in Martinique in 1848, after the emancipation in Britain in 1833. The eruption of Mount Pelée on May 8, 1902, was a really important catastrophic moment in Martinique's history that destroyed Saint-Pierre, killing almost 30,000 inhabitants and leaving alive only one prisoner. Today, Martinique is a fascinating island where history and culture come together in a perfect blend of dense, foggy rainforest and mountain trails to scintillating beaches and busy markets. Whether trekking through its dramatic landscapes or indulging in its gastronomic pleasures, the heritage of Martinique is one of a kind.

Landscape and Climate

Martinique lies between the Atlantic Ocean on the east and the Caribbean Sea on the west. It forms part of the Windward Islands, with an indented coast; thus, no point is over seven miles from the sea. It has a chain consisting of three main massifs: Mount Pelée in the north, the Carbet Mountains in the center, and Mount Vauclin in the south, giving it a highland terrain. The island is climatically tropical, hot, and humid, with average temperatures from 23 to 30 °C. The trade winds somewhat moderate the climate, though Martinique is storm- and cyclone-prone from June to October of the rainy season. The island also has three tourist seasons: the peak, from December to April. Martinique has something to amuse almost every kind of traveler. The northern part, for the hiker or naturalist, comprises mountains and rainforests with an endearing array of flora and fauna. The southern part offers excellent shopping and relaxing on beaches. In this way, Martinique has become an intriguing combination of historical import, cultural variety, and natural beauty.

Seasons and Best Time to Visit Martinique

This beautiful Caribbean gem has a diverse climate that brings distinct experiences depending on when you visit. Let's break down the seasons and help you plan your perfect trip.

High Season: December to April

This is the peak time to visit Martinique. The weather is wonderfully warm and dry, making it ideal for beach lovers and sunseekers. However, be prepared for higher prices and larger crowds, as this is when most tourists flock to the island. Hotels and flights can be pricey, so booking early is wise.

Low Season: May to November

During this period, Europeans often head back home, taking advantage of pleasant weather and varied travel opportunities closer to them. For Martinique, this time brings fewer tourists and lower prices. If you want to enjoy the island without the hustle and bustle, May and June are excellent months to visit. The weather is still lovely, with dry conditions and manageable humidity.

Summer and Cyclone Season: July to November

Summers in Martinique are hot and humid, and you might encounter some rain. But don't let the term "cyclone season" scare you away. While there is a higher chance of rain, the weather remains generally pleasant. Sightseeing can still be a joy, and the lush landscapes are a treat. Just be cautious if you're planning a trip in September, as the likelihood of hurricanes and tropical storms increases.

Our Recommendation:

For a perfect blend of good weather, fewer crowds, and lower costs, aim for May or June. You'll enjoy dry, comfortable conditions and more affordable travel expenses. If you don't mind the humidity and occasional rain, July and August are also great months to explore Martinique's rich culture and natural beauty.

Planning Your Trip

Martinique is surprisingly easy to reach. You can fly directly from major hubs in the US, Canada, and Europe. And for island hopping, ferries connect Martinique to its Caribbean neighbors.

Getting there

Air Travel

Most visitors touch down at Martinique Aimé Césaire International Airport, which connects the island to various destinations in the Caribbean, Europe, North America, and beyond. If you're traveling from mainland France, you only need a national ID card. However, if your flight has a layover in another country, make sure to carry your passport.

By Boat

Martinique is a popular stop for cruise ships, especially during the high season. Large ships usually dock in Fort-de-France harbor, with shuttles available to take you to the heart of the action. For a more intimate arrival, smaller vessels dock closer to town. Ferries from neighboring islands like Guadeloupe, Dominica, and Saint Lucia, operated by companies such as **Express des Iles**, are also excellent options for hopping over to Martinique.

Companies like Express des Iles are your go to. Check them out online at **express-des-iles.com.**

Entry Requirements

1. **EU Citizens and Residents:** Since Martinique is part of the European Union, citizens of EU member states, as well as Iceland, Norway, Liechtenstein, and Switzerland, can enter with just a valid ID card. You can stay as long as you want and even seek employment without any additional paperwork.

2. **Non-EU Citizens:** Martinique is not part of the Schengen Area, so there are specific entry requirements:

   o If you do not need a visa for the Schengen Area, you can visit Martinique visa-free for up to 90 days.

   o Schengen visas do not apply here. If you need a visa for the Schengen Area, you must get a separate visa for Martinique from a French consulate.

3. **US and Canadian Citizens:** No visa is needed for stays up to 90 days, just bring a valid passport.

4. **Other Nationalities:** If you're from countries like Argentina, Australia, Japan, Mexico, or South Korea, a valid passport will suffice for short stays. However, if your country isn't on the visa-exempt list, you'll need to secure a visa before your trip.

Additional Tips

- **Return Ticket:** Ensure you have a return or onward ticket, as you might be asked to show proof at the airport.

- **Stay Duration:** If you're planning to stay longer, check if you need to extend your visa or apply for a different type.

Visa-exempt list

Argentina, Guatemala, Vatican City, Venezuela, Honduras, Japan, Australia, Croatia, El Salvador, Malta, Mexico, New Zealand, Nicaragua, Panama, Paraguay, San Marino, South Korea, Bulgaria, Brunei, Canada, Chile, Costa Rica, Singapore, Uruguay, United States.

Getting Around

Traveling around Martinique is an absolutely delightful experience, with several convenient options available to suit the needs of any traveler.

By Car

Renting a car gives an opportunity for comfortable travel and pacing through various Martinique landscapes and hidden corners. The agencies providing this service are rather numerous, particularly in Fort-de-France. The island's road network is pretty good, though sometimes the roads can be serpentine and steep; a car will be quite handy when traveling these roads.

Taxis

While driving gives a feeling of freedom, another efficient and culturally rich way to travel is by using the collective taxis—locally called "**taxicos.**" These Shared taxis are a cornerstone in Martinique's public transport system, connecting all the communes on the island. Operating every day, except on **Sundays, from 6 a.m. to 6 p.m.**, taxicos are an authentic, cheaper way to get around and mix with the locals. The traditional taxis are more expensive and less efficient than taxicos.

Bus

For those who would not like to drive, the limited bus network serves the southwestern part of the island, including the key areas between Trois-Ilets and Sainte-Anne. In the north and center, though, services are sparse, so you may want to plan accordingly if you're relying on public transportation.

By Boat

For a scenic and leisurely commute, consider taking a shuttle boat, especially between Fort-de-France and the resort areas. The shuttle boats generally run every 30 minutes and offer views not available on road travel without any traffic concerns. Service usually stops between 5:45 pm and 8 pm depending on the day, so be sure to check the schedule.

Windward Islands are among the companies through which one can charter boats to extend the adventure into Caribbean waters outside Martinique Island. This is quite an exciting option for taking tours around the islands by both crewed and bareboat charters.

Cruise lines

Martinique also features as one of the popular cruise destinations. Major cruise lines often include Fort-de-France in their itinerary, hence allowing passengers to participate in the cruise without prior elaborate planning. The proximity of the cruise terminal to downtown allows for easy excursions and the discovery of the charm of the island.

The Guide - Martinique

Fort de France

Fort-de-France is a dynamic capital of Martinique, where French charm meets the exuberance of the Caribbean. The largest city on this island encompasses all ranges of culture, heavy with liveliness; its center is usually bustling up to a quaint seaside promenade. Here, one finds rows of bars and restaurants, quintessentially French in atmosphere, where one can either have a leisurely meal or a refreshing drink with a view.

Photo by Wil ZAID (Unsplash)

The imposing Fort Saint-Louis, a historic 17th-century fortress in the heart of the city, testifies to the rich history of the island. Then there is "The Savannah" or La Savane, a beautiful park full of tropical trees providing a peaceful oasis at the heart of the city. To the east, the port area goes into frenetic activity with the cruise ships and merchant vessels that begin to dock, bringing a steady tide of visitors and goods to the island.

Understanding a little bit of the history behind Fort-de-France helps set it into context. This was made the capital in 1902, following the destruction of the former capital of Saint Pierre by the eruption of Mount Pelée. Nowadays, Fort-de-France has grown significantly, now home to nearly 150,000 residents and expanding to the surrounding hills and plains, including the area where the airport is situated.

Photo by Crobard (Getty)

Getting There

Fort-de-France is relatively easy to reach, especially through the Aimé Cesaire International Airport in the suburb of Le Lamentin. Those who enjoy traveling by sea will find that the city's harbor is visited frequently enough by cruise ships to make this a reasonable mode of arrival as well.

Getting Around

Once in Fort-de-France, getting around is pretty easy. There's a good bus service operating daily from 6 am to 8:30 pm, including on Sundays and holidays. Remember that no cash is taken on the buses; purchase your tickets using the MT Ticket Mobile App or at a store.

  MT Ticket Mobile App

Other convenient means of transportation include taxis that run at any time of day. One can also rent a moped or car, for more mobility-if one is planning to travel beyond the city center.

Tourist Attractions

Jardin de Balata

Garden

 [Rte de Balata, Fort-de-France 97234, Martinique](#)

Opening Hours: 9:00 AM - 6:00 PM

Tour duration: 1 – 2 hours

You won't want to miss the breathtaking Le Jardin de Balata, a tropical paradise just a short drive from Fort-de-France along the scenic Trace route, which also leads to the historic town of Saint Pierre. This lush garden, created by the passionate horticulturist Jean-Philippe Thoze, is a botanical haven that showcases an extraordinary variety of tropical plants and flowers. As you step into the Jardin de Balata, you'll be greeted by a meticulously maintained garden, adorned with a stunning variety of tropical plants. At the entrance, you'll find a quaint house that once belonged to the garden's original owners. Here, you can learn about the history and vision of Jean-Philippe Thoze, who also designed the gardens at the local zoo.

Photo by Gary Killian.

Stroll through the garden and enjoy the sight of vibrant plants and blooming flowers. You'll come across two ponds filled with lively fish and a walking bridge that offers a slight thrill with its gentle swaying. The aerial path provides a unique bird's-eye view of the gardens and surrounding hills, a feature that many visitors find exhilarating. While the garden is not overflowing with flowers, the blooming plants and the serene ambiance more than make up for it. The tour typically lasts about 1.5 hours, and while guided tours provide rich insights into the flora, you can also explore independently if you prefer a quicker visit.

Photo by Weronika (Unsplash)

Insider Tips

Beat the Crowds: To enjoy a quieter exploration, especially during the off-season, arrive as soon as the garden opens at 9 a.m. This way, you can avoid the cruise groups that typically arrive later in the day.

Weekday Experience: If your schedule allows, visit on a weekday to experience fewer crowds than on weekends or holidays.

Budget Check: Admission can be a bit pricey, especially during peak times. Keep this in mind when planning your visit.

Hummingbird Paradise: Near the entrance, don't miss the feeders where you can watch enchanting hummingbirds darting about, adding a magical touch to your visit.

Practical Tips

Parking: The journey to Jardin de Balata involves navigating a winding road and finding parking can be a bit of a challenge, so plan to arrive early.

Dining: To cap off your visit, consider booking a table at the nearby restaurant, La Luciole, which offers delightful meals in a picturesque setting.

Fort Saint-Louis

Historical site

Opening hours: 9:00 am – 1:00 pm

Tour Duration: 1-2 hours

 [JW3M+2C6, Fort-de-France 97200, Martinique](#)

Located in the heart of Fort de France, Fort Saint-Louis is an impressive part of the history of Martinique, offering a fascinating glimpse of the past and present of the island. Originally built from wood in 1680 and later transformed into a formidable "Vauban" form, the fort was born after Louis XIV, the patron saint of Fort-de-France. Fort Saint-Louis is not only a historic monument, but it is an active naval base and headquarters of the French Navy in Antilles. Because of its operational status, only guided tours are allowed, making it a truly interesting experience.

Tours from Tuesday to Saturday, from 9 am to 1 pm, are offered in French and English, costing €8 for adults and €4 for children aged 6-14. Be sure to wear comfortable walking shoes and stop at the tourist office at **29 Victor Hugo Street** to buy tickets. Visitors rave about the impressive views of the bay of Flamands and the impressive architecture of the fortress. Friendly guides provide a rich historical context, making the two-hour trip educational and enjoyable. Although parts of the fortress are restricted, accessible areas offer sufficient value for its strategic importance and breathtaking beauty.

Photo by LanaCanada (Getty)

The exploration of Fort Saint-Louis is like entering a different era, but the lively atmosphere of Fort-de-France keeps you in the present. After your visit, stroll along the lovely harbour front with street vendors or relax at the small beach next to the fort. Whether you're a history lover or just looking for a local culture to indulge in, Fort Saint-Louis is a must visit destination in Martinique.

St. Louis Cathédral

Religious site

[Rue Victor Schoelcher, Fort-de-France 97200, Martinique](#)

Come and visit this atypical iron building-the St. Louis Cathedral-richly impressive and bearing important features of religious life on Martinique Island. If not solely a house of worship, this cathedral is in and of itself a historical treasure that carries in its stones the architectural and cultural spirit of Fort-de-France.

Photo by Thierry64 (Getty)

The history of St Louis Cathedral began in 1671 when the first place of worship at Fort-Royal was nothing more than a straw-covered shelter. Today's building constructed in 1891, joins a neo-Gothic exterior with a Roman-Byzantine interior, very much the fashion at the time. Its frame is totally of metal to withstand earthquakes and is 66 meters in length by 24 meters in width.

The steeple will be visible as you get closer, and you may hear the bells ringing in the distance, which heightens the excitement of your visit. Despite its modest size, the inside is exquisitely furnished, creating a lovely setting for introspection and adoration. But keep in mind that the cathedral only accepts euros, so it's a good idea to have some on hand to prevent any misunderstanding. St. Louis Cathedral is a great place to stop when seeing Fort-de-France because it's near to the park La Savane and only a 30-minute walk from the cruise terminal. The well-kept and free cathedral provides a tranquil haven in the middle of the busy metropolis. For those who enjoy history and beautiful architecture, it is a true thrill.

Tips for Your Visit

- **Currency:** Bring Euros to purchase candles or make donations.

- **Timing:** Visit early to enjoy the serene environment before it gets too busy, especially around Passover.

- **Accessibility:** The walk from the cruise terminal is scenic and enjoyable, perfect for those looking to explore the city on foot.

Schoelcher Library

Tourist site

 [1 Rue de la liberté, Fort-de-France 97200, Martinique](#)

Entry fee: Free

A visit to the Schoelcher Library in Fort-de-France is tantamount to a visit to history, wrapped in really nice architecture. Conceived and constructed in 1887 by the architect Pierre-Henri Picq in Paris, this icon of a library was dismantled, shipped to Martinique, and assembled on the edge of La Savane Park. It takes the name from Victor Schoelcher, one of the earliest and most outstanding abolitionists, who left his 10,000 books and 250 scores of music to this library on one condition it shall always be free for all.

Its bright, exotic façade really stands out in Fort-de-France's cityscape and visitors will be drawn to it. Inside, you'll find soaring archways, intricate ironwork, and spacious reading rooms. While its exterior beauty hypnotizes many, the interior is not as well-preserved as it used to be, though this building still has historical charm. Entry is free of charge, so it's a good place for a look around while doing a town walk or for rest during a cruise excursion. From an architectural standpoint to a historical curiosity, or simply for a breath of cool air, the Schoelcher Library is an aesthetically pleasing and culturally diverse building, a man's tribute to equality in knowledge.

Grand Marche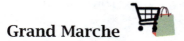

Shopping center

 [Rue Blenac, Fort-de-France 97200, Martinique](#)

Opening hours: 6:00 am – 4 :00pm

Saturday: 6:00 am – 1:00pm

Sunday: closed

Welcome to Grand Marché, an open-air market that's a feast for the senses. This bustling hub, just a 10-minute walk from the cruise ship, offers a delightful array of experiences for locals and tourists alike. As you stroll through, you'll encounter fruit stands brimming with fresh produce, aromatic bakeries, and vibrant stalls selling an assortment of souvenirs.

Grand Marché is perfect for picking up unique souvenirs, from purses and thermos bottles to spices and artisan crafts. While the market has a great selection, savvy shoppers might want to explore the parallel streets where similar items can be found at lower prices.

Culinary Highlights

One of the market's standout features is its culinary offerings. Don't miss the two fantastic restaurants upstairs, where you can savor local delicacies. These eateries also provide convenient restrooms downstairs in the middle, right by the stairs, making your visit even more comfortable. For a real treat, try the rum punch at one of the market's restaurants—it certainly lives up to its name! Besides the punch, you'll find a wide range of local jams, honey, and an impressive variety of rums and liqueurs.

Timing and Practical Tips

A word of advice: the market often gets into full swing later than the official opening time, around 11:30 AM. So, take your time and perhaps start your day with a leisurely breakfast before heading over. Also, remember that while many items have French labels, having a translation app handy can enhance your shopping experience.

Restaurants at the market (few mention)

Chez Geneviève

> ➤ **Price range:** $$ - $$$

Chez Hector

> ➤ **Price range:** $$ - $$$

La Savane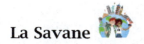

Park

 [JW3J+6XF, Fort-de-France 97200, Martinique](#)

La Savane Park in Fort-de-France is the city's lively green heart and a great stop if you're exploring Martinique on foot or coming from the cruise port. This expansive five-hectare park, known historically as the "Jardin du Roy," has come a long way from its military roots as a training ground for Fort Saint-Louis soldiers. Now, it's a scenic urban oasis bordered by royal palms, travelers' trees, and vibrant bougainvillea, and it stretches from Fort Saint-Louis right into the city's core.

Photo by falco (Pixabay)

On Sundays, you might find local events like horse shows or even marathons filling the park with festive energy, music, and food stalls—perfect for joining in on the island vibe. The park is also a romantic spot for locals, and it's lined with snack kiosks and souvenir stalls. Plus, it connects beautifully to the beach at Plage de la Française, making it an ideal place to relax, stroll, or enjoy a seaside break. Though it's more about the atmosphere than any standout monuments, La Savane is a fun, open space worth exploring for an authentic slice of Fort-de-France life.

Distillerie la Favorite

Rum distillery

 [5,5km Route de Lamentin, Le Lamentin 97232, Martinique](#)

Nestled right in the heart of Martinique is Distillerie la Favorite, which offers a leap into the past. In contrast to high-tech, commercialized distilleries, La Favorite still has its original charm and traditional ways of making rum. Immediately upon entering this small distillery, one is thrust into an authentic, raw factory environment where history and craftsmanship finally come together.

Many visitors usually begin their tour by viewing the entire process of rum-making. You can observe the whole process, from loading and crushing sugar cane to filling the tanks with juice. The highlight is represented by the operational distillation columns, with the very well-thought-out process starting from sugar cane all the way to fine rum. What one can definitely experience uniquely at La Favorite is tasting rum directly from the column at an impressive 88% alcohol, which is both surprising and deliciously candy-like for the amateurs.

The modest shop at the distillery falls right amid their range of high-quality rums. This is an absolute must, thanks to the attentive staff who take you through the tasting of the different varieties so that you can appreciate their craftsmanship. From the welcome glass of icy rum, this visit often becomes a memorable one-what with great rum and informative panels peppered here and there within the distillery.

In fact, La Favorite stands out because of its adherence to tradition and machinery. This distillery is a connoisseur's haven, an oasis for the appreciation of how things used to be done to rums. The rum tasting at the end of this visit will be a treat for your palate but also a deeper understanding of how this distillery creates its product uniquely.

La Boucle d'Absalon

Hike trail

 [MWH4+8C, Fort-de-France 97200, Martinique](MWH4+8C,_Fort-de-France_97200,_Martinique)

La Boucle d'Absalon is one of those intruiging trails in Martinique that mingles natural beauty with challenging terrain. Although the trail is usually advertised as a 2-hour loop, for those who are not seasoned hikers, it will usually take more time. This trail is especially famous for its first steep climb, which may be really tiring, particurlaly when the path turns all muddy after rainfall. Steep to begin with, it will leave you breathless; it may be slippery, muddy in some parts, and requires proper footwear. Once you pass the climb, one immediately gets introduced to lush tropical vegetation and some great viewpoints thereafter.

The path then winds through the forest, offering a peaceful retreat away from the more touristy spots. Along the way, there is a beautiful waterfall where one can cool off and even dip one's feet in the water; thus, it is also a wonderful place to rest. This loop teems with life, from several species of birds and lizards, while various types of plant life add to the charm of the trail.

Even though it's pretty demanding, La Boucle d'Absalon can become family-friendly if the kids aren't too scared of adventure, while certain parts may allow group activities more easily. The hike starts from the old baths, where hot springs and a bathtub for rinsing can still be seen. This gives a fantastic view of Fort de France from the top and finishes in steps through to a stone bridge, which is the most picturesque end to your adventure.

Culinary

Savor the Gastronomic Fusion in Fort-de-France

Fort-de-France is a culinary melting pot where African, Caribbean, Indian, and European flavors converge. Among these dishes that one must try whenever exploring the city are **boudin noir** (blood sausage), **crabes farcis** (stuffed crabs), **colombo de poulet pimenté** (spicy chicken curry), and **accras de poisson croustillants** (crispy fish fritters). Here are some must-try dishes:

Chatrou: A hearty octopus stew with tomatoes, onions, and an array of herbs.

Fricassée de lambi: A conch stew bursting with island flavors.

Colombo: A rich curry made with chicken, lamb, or veggies, simmered in spicy coconut milk.

Accras de Morue: Delicious cod fritters, best enjoyed hot with a dipping sauce.

Sorbet Coco: A cool and creamy coconut sorbet, perfect for a tropical day.

Rum Lover's Paradise

Rum is king in Martinique. Visit distilleries like **Distillerie JM, Habitation Clément,** or **La Favorite** to see the rum-making process and enjoy tastings. Don't miss:

- **Rhum Vieux**: Aged rum, perfect for sipping straight or in a cocktail.

- **Ti' Punch:** The quintessential Martinican drink made with rum, lime, and a bit of sugar.

Where to Eat in Fort-de-France

Fort-de-France offers a range of dining options to suit every budget:

1. **Chez Carole** - Caribbean - $

   ➢ Small and intimate, with a limited menu. Carole is recognized for her warm hospitality and delicious seafood meals.

2. **Galanga Fish Bar** - Caribbean - $$ - $$$

   ➢ Highly recommended for its excellent cuisine and setting. Try the **filet de côte de veau.**

3. **Kay Ali** - French - $$$$

   ➢ This vegetarian restaurant, located on the outskirts of Fort-de-France, is one of the best in the city.

4. **LA LUCIOLE** - French, Caribbean - $$ - $$$

   ➢ Known for exquisite food and a convenient location near the Balata Gardens.

5. **The Yellow** - French, Caribbean - $$$$

   ➢ Provides excellent cuisine and service. Don't miss the vegetarian options and fruit-based desserts.

6. **Miza** - French, Caribbean - $$$$

> A beautiful culinary discovery with a diverse menu.

7. **Restaurant Le Hanoï** - Chinese, Asian - $

   > For more than 15 years, it has been well-known for its generous food serving quantities and consistent high quality.

8. **Djol Dou** - Caribbean - $$ - $$$

   > Ideal for home-cooked Creole dishes. A favorite spot for locals and tourists alike.

For more restaurants in fort de France... check here

Budget-Friendly Options

In Martinique, you can find a good meal for around 20 euros or less at small, family-run eateries. Mid-range restaurants offer set menus from 20 to 30 euros, while high-end dining can go up to 40 euros or more for a set meal.

Eating out is generally more affordable at lunch than dinner, and many restaurants offer kids' menus, making dining a pleasant experience for families.

Where to Stay

Fort-de-France, the vibrant heart of Martinique! Located right at the hub of the island, this city offers you a great cultural experience, a feeling of excellent food, and breathtaking scenery. Staying in Fort-de-France keeps you right at the heart of the action with easy access to an array of bars, restaurants, and fascinating museums, which include the Martinique Departmental Museum, the Père Pinchon Museum, and the Aimé Césaire Museum Space.

Hôtel Pelican

Located in the nearby town of Schoelcher, the Hôtel Pelican provides a serene escape while still being close to the action in Fort-de-France. Enjoy the relaxing ambiance and the beautiful surroundings in this half-board hotel.

L'Impératrice

Step back in time with a stay at L'Impératrice. This charming half-board hotel exudes old-world elegance and offers a unique experience right in the center of Fort-de-France.

Bayfront Hotel

Another excellent choice in Fort-de-France, the Bayfront Hotel provides stunning waterfront views and comfortable accommodations. This half-board hotel is perfect for those who want to stay close to the sea.

Karibea Valmeniere Hotel

This half-board hotel is a fantastic choice for those looking for a blend of luxury and convenience. With a rooftop pool offering stunning views of the city, the Karibea Valmeniere Hotel ensures a memorable stay.

Carib Hotel

Located in the heart of Fort-de-France, the Carib Hotel offers comfortable accommodations with easy access to local attractions. This half-board hotel ensures you have a hassle-free stay with meals included.

Simon Hotel

A modern gem in Fort-de-France, the Simon Hotel boasts stylish rooms and top-notch amenities. Perfect for travelers who appreciate contemporary comfort and convenience, this half-board hotel keeps you close to all the city's best spots.

For lodging and booking check....

Itinerary

7-Day Itinerary for Fort-de-France, Martinique

Welcome to the vibrant heart of Martinique! This 7-day itinerary is designed to help you experience the best of what this beautiful city has to offer. From lush gardens and historic sites to local markets and serene parks, Fort-de-France has something for everyone. Let's dive in!

Day 1: Arrival and Getting Acquainted

Upon arriving at Aimé Cesaire International Airport in Le Lamentin or docking at the Fort-de-France harbor via cruise ship, you can check in to your chosen accommodation, such as Hôtel Pelican, L'Impératrice, Bayfront Hotel, Karibea Valmeniere Hotel, Carib Hotel, or Simon Hotel. After settling in, take a leisurely stroll through La Savane Park, a central green space where you can stretch your legs and soak in the local atmosphere, complete with snack kiosks and souvenir stalls. As evening falls, make your way to Chez Carole for a delicious and budget-friendly Caribbean dinner, marking the start of your culinary adventure in Martinique.

Day 2: Gardens and History

Start your day with a visit to the breathtaking Jardin de Balata, where you can beat the crowds and immerse yourself in the serene ambiance of the lush tropical gardens and unique aerial pathways. After exploring the gardens, enjoy a delightful meal at La Luciole, which offers picturesque views to complement your dining experience. In the afternoon, make your way to the historic Fort Saint-Louis, where joining a guided tour allows you to delve into its fascinating history while enjoying stunning views of the bay. As the sun sets, conclude your day with a delicious seafood dinner at Galanga Fish Bar, savoring the fresh flavors that perfectly round off your memorable outing.

Day 3: Cultural Exploration

Start your day by visiting the magnificent St. Louis Cathedral, where you can admire its neo-Gothic architecture and the serene beauty of its interior; it's a perfect opportunity to light a candle or make a donation. In the afternoon, continue your exploration at the iconic Schoelcher Library, whose bright and exotic façade invites you in to appreciate the rich history contained within its walls, all accessible with free entry, making it a highlight of your city walk. As the evening approaches, indulge in a fine dining experience at Kay Ali, where you can savor exquisite French cuisine and conclude your day with a touch of elegance.

Day 4: Market Day and Rum Tasting

Start your day at the vibrant Grand Marché, where you can explore an array of fresh produce, delightful bakeries, and unique souvenirs. Be sure to indulge in the local delicacies served at the market's restaurants. After soaking in the market's atmosphere, head to Distillerie la Favorite in the afternoon for an insightful tour of the traditional rum-making process, complete with a tasting session to savor the flavors. As the day winds down, indulge in a delicious meal at LA LUCIOLE, a nearby restaurant that beautifully blends French and Caribbean cuisine for a memorable dining experience.

Day 5: Outdoor Adventures

Start your day by embarking on a hike along La Boucle d'Absalon, where you'll be immersed in beautiful tropical scenery and have the opportunity to spot local wildlife. Don't forget to wear proper footwear and bring plenty of water to stay hydrated. After your invigorating hike, unwind at Plage de la Française, a charming beach conveniently located near La Savane Park. As evening approaches, treat yourself to a delightful dining experience at The Yellow, where you can savor a delicious mix of French and Caribbean flavors, perfectly capping off your adventurous day.

Day 6: Exploring Beyond the City

Start your day with a trip to the historic town of Saint Pierre, where you can explore the captivating ruins and delve into its rich and fascinating history. After a morning of discovery, take a break for lunch at a local restaurant, indulging in the regional specialties while enjoying the charming atmosphere that the town has to offer. In the evening, make your way back to Fort-de-France and treat yourself to dinner at Miza, where you can savor an exquisite blend of French and Caribbean dishes, perfectly capping off your delightful day trip.

Day 7: Last-Minute Exploration and Departure

On your final morning in Fort-de-France, take the opportunity to explore the bustling streets around Grand Marché, searching for the perfect souvenirs and unique gifts. Afterward, return to your accommodation to relax and pack, reflecting on the memorable week you've spent in Martinique, enjoying a moment of tranquility before the journey home. For your last dinner, savor delicious Asian cuisine at Restaurant Le Hanoï, relishing the flavors as you reminisce about your adventures. When the moment comes to depart, head to the airport or harbor, carrying with you wonderful memories of your time in this vibrant city, or set off on another journey to discover the beauty of other bustling places in Martinique.

Sainte Anne

Sainte-Anne, Martinique—the Pearl Nestled in the southernmost part of Martinique, Sainte-Anne is a treasure trove of natural beauty and reminiscences of cultural history. With an area stretching along a span of 22 kilometers of stunning coastline, this commune hosts some of the most beautiful beaches in the Lesser Antilles. The landscape is a charming combination of coconut groves, savannahs, and serene ponds—a true Eldorado for lovers of nature.

A Vast Past

Sainte-Anne epitomizes Martinique's history: the Arawaks, the Carib Indians, and then the Europeans settled here in succession. This has been and is a scene of much bloodshed-English and French alike fought for this island. Sainte-Anne takes its name from a commander who defended it against the English in 1808. Whereas sugar cane was the lifeblood of the local economy, tourism has taken over today, and accommodations run the gamut from cozy homestays to luxurious villas.

Photo by life for stock

Must-See Monuments

The sugar industry has left quite a few poignants around the region: the ruins of Crève-Cœur. It is a listed historic monument of 1992, comprising the manor and workers' village with its industrial buildings at the end of the 18th century.

The Church of Our Lady of Sainte-Anne was built first in the 18th century, and as cyclones have destroyed parts of it, it was rebuilt again and again. It is classified as a historic monument and embodies a unique mixture of architectural styles.

Another highlight is the Ilet Cabrit Lighthouse, reachable from Salines Beach. This striking lighthouse with its metal tower, erected since 1929, keeps company with the old caretaker's house, showing the maritime life of this beautiful island.

A visit to the Moulin Val d'Or is a voyage right in the middle of Sainte-Anne's past. The old sugar mill from the 17th century is animated with costumed-style, following the traditional method of producing sugar.

Dream Beaches

No visit to Sainte-Anne is complete without seeing its world-famous beaches. Salines Beach is the crown gem, separated into three sections: Grande Anse, Petite Anse, and Grande Terre. Known for its pristine white sand and tranquil, turquoise seas, it's a favorite with both visitors and residents.

For a calmer, more private experience, travel to Anse Michel near Cap Chevalier. This beach is recognized for its untouched beauty and bright coral reefs, great for snorkeling and kitesurfing aficionados.

If you're seeking seclusion, Anse Trabaud is the place to be. This practically empty beach, lying between the cliffs of Pointe de l'Enfer and Pointe de Baham, provides 2 kilometers of beautiful sand and peaceful waves. Be advised that naturism is permitted here, so you may meet beachgoers embracing the natural surroundings fully.

Natural Wonders

The Savane des Pétrifications forms one such savannah of arid beauty, born from ancient volcanic eruptions in the Martinique Regional Natural Park. The name refers to the now-gone petrified trees that dotted the landscape but have since vanished. Hikers will be able to experience this unique desert-like terrain on the famous Trace des Caps trail.

Next to it, there is the protected area of the Etang des Salines with the coastal forest and its valuable mangrove ecosystem. By means of a boardway path, guests can master this wonder of nature and get a glimpse of very special local flora and fauna. The Réserve Naturelle des îlets de Sainte-Anne can be reached only by boat and provides an important breeding site for seabirds, thus a certain paradise for all avid birdwatchers.

Getting There

Getting to Sainte-Anne is easy. The airport serving Martinique is the Martinique Aimé Césaire International Airport, located in Le Lamentin. From this airport, Sainte-Anne lies southward about an hour's drive away. Public transportations aren't quite common here, so you will need to rent a car. This venture lets you explore the island at your own pace and comfort.

Getting Around

At Sainte-Anne, once you have arrived, the best way of getting around will be by car. In such a way, you can easily reach all those wonderful beaches, historical sites, and natural parks. Biking is a great idea for shorter journeys because you can get a wonderful view of the scenery. Alternatively, if you don't drive, you could take taxis, but it would be expensive (**€55 - €110**).

Tourist attractions

Plage des Salines

Beach

 [97227, Martinique](#)

Discover the charm of Plage des Salines, one of Martinique's most beloved beaches! Picture yourself on soft white sands, under swaying palm trees, with calm, turquoise waters gently lapping at the shore. This idyllic spot is perfect for soaking up the Caribbean sun. To fully enjoy your visit, plan to arrive early in the morning (8:00 am) to secure a prime spot before the crowds. Weekends and peak seasons can be bustling, so if you prefer a more relaxed atmosphere, try visiting midweek or early in the day.

Plage des Salines offers everything you need for a perfect beach day. The gentle slope makes it ideal for young children, and the abundant shade from coconut trees provides a perfect escape from the sun. Enjoy delicious Creole specialties, refreshing drinks, and even ice cream from the on-site restaurants. If you prefer a picnic, feel free to bring your own food. Deckchairs are available for rent, adding a touch of comfort to your day.

Parking can be challenging, so arriving early is crucial, especially during holidays and school vacations. Don't miss the chance to sip fresh coconut water or savor the local cuisine at the beachfront restaurants.

Photo by mrsiraphol

Whether you visit in the low season **(month of May)** with just a handful of people or during busier times, Plage des Salines offers a beautiful and tranquil setting. The clear, warm waters are perfect for swimming, and the expansive beach ensures there's plenty of room for everyone to find their perfect spot.

Savane des Pétrifications

Nature and wildlife

 [Savane des Pétrifications, Sainte-Anne 97227, Martinique](#)

Tucked at the end of the road in Sainte-Anne, the Savane des Pétrifications offers a rare glimpse into Martinique's prehistoric charm with its surreal, desert-like landscape by the sea. This hike is an adventurer's delight, taking you through an otherworldly terrain of fascinating rock formations, colorful chalcedony, red jasper, and even traces of petrified wood. It's like stepping into a natural museum where geology fans will feel right at home (but remember, collecting is a big no-no!).

This trail is perfect for a family outing, with plenty of crabs and sweeping views to keep everyone entertained. Bring lots of water, sturdy shoes, and sunscreen – the heat here can be intense, so aim to start your walk early. The route also includes a quirky little bridge crossing over the river, but don't be surprised if it's more for decoration than use; at high tide, you might need to wade across!

With minimal signage and a rugged road in, the journey to the Savane may feel a bit remote, but it only adds to the excitement. It's a hike full of surprises, ending with a stunning view that's well worth the effort.

La Pointe Marin

Beach

 [Martinique](#)

Welcome to La Pointe Marin also known as Plage de Pointe Marin, a stunning beach destination in Martinique. This guide will help you make the most of your visit to this beautiful and bustling beach. La Pointe Marin is a long, curved beach with easy access offering plenty of shade, making it perfect for a relaxing day under the sun. The beach features calm waters, ideal for children, and it's a great spot for families. This beach can be crowded especially on weekends, so visiting early during weekdays is ideal, allowing you to fully enjoy the serene environment. Amenities include a large parking lot, with a small fee being quite reasonable, and nearby restaurants and bars, including those near Club Med, which offer delicious local cuisine and refreshing drinks. There are plenty of shaded spots perfect for a break from the sun, especially needed during weekends when the beach can get quite crowded. The beach boasts beautiful white sand, turquoise waters, and postcard-worthy landscapes, with a gentle slope into the water that makes it safe and enjoyable for children.

Tips for Visiting

- **Timing:** To avoid the crowds, especially on weekends, head to the far right end of the beach, which tends to be less crowded.

- **Facilities:** Note the campsite located a few meters away, ideal for those looking to extend their stay.

- **Local Culture:** The people in Martinique are friendly and always willing to help. Don't hesitate to ask for directions or recommendations.

Things to Keep in Mind

While La Pointe Marin is a beautiful beach, it can get quite crowded, and in some areas, space might be limited. Despite this, the stunning scenery and friendly locals make it worth the visit.

Photo by Teddy Charti (Unsplash)

Anse Michel

Beach

 [C5PF+VFM, Sainte-Anne 97227, Martinique](#)

Anse Michel is a gem of Martinique's coastline, offering a bit of everything: shady palms, pristine sands, and a charming tropical vibe that feels like paradise. Upon arrival, you'll be greeted by a breathtaking view that's postcard-worthy, framed by tall, graceful palms and turquoise waters. The beach is ideal for relaxing in the shade with vendors nearby selling local treats and drinks—perfect for a day-long escape. However, be prepared for some wind here, which makes it a popular spot for kite and wind surfers. Watching them glide across the waves adds to the beach's lively atmosphere.

You'll take a short, scenic path through mangroves to reach Anse Michel. The ample, well-marked parking lot is a nice bonus, as parking can be rare in Martinique's more popular areas. Once you're there, take a short swim to explore two small, beautiful islets just off the shore. The closest one is suitable for most swimmers, but you'll need to be a strong swimmer to reach the further islet.

Although the beach sometimes faces sargassum seaweed invasions, the views and ambiance are so worth it, making Anse Michel a must-visit for any Martinique itinerary.

Photo by Claire ANSART (Pixabay)

Etang des Salines

Nature and bodies of water

 [Sainte-Anne 97227, Martinique](#)

Nestled just behind the popular Salines Beach, the Etang des Salines offers a quiet sojourn into nature, ideal for quiet exploration amidst the vibrant landscapes of Martinique. This saltwater lake along the coast is one of the less-known attractions that invites visitors to delve into its unique ecosystem through an easily accessible boardwalk.

Among the specific charms of the visit to Étang des Salines is the easy, quiet time on the wooden path. You can also be practically alone on the pontoon, with soothing and constant sounds of nature. The walk is relaxing and instructive, and at the same time, the panels are well-made, showing captivating insights into the salt pond ecology. Such easily readable explanations immediately allow each guest, from casual visitors to amateurs of nature, to appreciate the enormous variety of flora and fauna. It is a home for wildlife; in fact, there are thousands of crabs among the mangroves.

As you walk along this track, you will get plenty of chances to see these fascinating animals close up. The boardwalk consists of hides and information boards that provide a chance to learn more about the local flora and fauna. You may also come across locals fishing for crabs, which will add a cultural touch to your visit.

Photo by lifeforstock

Perfect for a Half-Day Adventure

Etang des Salines is ideally situated next to Salines Beach, making it a perfect place to merge nature exploration with beach enjoyment. You can easily spend half a day here, enjoying the beautiful weather while alternating between an informative tour of the lake and the lively beach atmosphere. The peacefulness of the pond provides a pleasant contrast to the energetic beach, creating a balanced experience.

Although parking can be somewhat challenging, the effort is definitely worthwhile. Visiting Etang des Salines enhances your trip to Salines Beach and gives you a distinctive look at the natural beauty of Martinique. For those interested in further exploration, a 40-minute walk along a nearby road to another parking area presents different flora and breathtaking ocean vistas.

Maya Beach Club

Aquatic activities

Plage de l, Anse Caritan, Sainte-Anne 97227, Martinique

Recommended time: 1 hour

The Maya Beach Club in Sainte-Anne is a perfect destination for a day of fun and relaxation. This nautical leisure hub features an array of giant inflatable games, including trampolines, gliders, climbing walls, and aqua volley, ensuring an exciting experience for visitors of all ages. It's a family-friendly spot where parents can join their children in the activities, resulting in a delightful time filled with laughter and a few playful falls.

While engaging in these activities, safety is a top priority, so life jackets are provided, and a lifeguard is always on duty.

Most people describe the sliding and jumping on the inflatables as both exhilarating and exhausting, but also leaving them with great memories. Although the beach is small and services for non-participants are limited to the adjacent snack bar, the atmosphere is cozy and welcoming. Guests can relax in a shaded areas, enjoying comfortable chairs and tables provided by the club. Culinary delights add to the charm, with appetizing salads served in bamboo containers and kid-friendly chicken and fried donuts. The Maya Beach Club offers a wonderful mix of action and relaxation, making it an ideal spot to kick off or conclude a visit to Sainte Anne, Martinique.

Anse Trabaud

Beach

 [Martinique](#)

Anse Trabaud is probably one of those virginal beaches located in Martinique that take quite a lot of effort to get to, that's if you're willing to make the trek. Indeed, the long stretches of golden sand, crystal waters, and untouched natural beauty make it perfect for those seeking a more remote beach experience. Getting here, though, is actually an adventure. Access can be a little difficult, the usual rough and bumpy road that may hold one or two surprises.

It's sometimes a 2 km path you may walk if the toll gate is closed. Access is via a road crossing private land; hence, there is sometimes a small fee for parking or entry. The beach is immense and has a peaceful, almost serene quality to it, with far fewer crowds than many of Martinique's more accessible spots.

Swimmers should note that the water current is strong; thus, it is best suited to confident swimmers. It's also partially naturist-friendly, though some visitors have noted a bit of voyeurism, so just be mindful. In short, Anse Trabaud is a real gem for people who want to enjoy Martinique in its most natural, wild mode. It surely unites a very special mix of beauty, serenity, and adventure.

Piton de Crêve Cœur

Mountain

 [Sainte-Anne 97227, Martinique](#)

Piton de Crêve Cœur is not just a hike but a lesson of history unto itself. The ascent is on one of the most ancient volcanoes in Martinique, and you'll run into remnants of the Habitation Crève-Coeur dating back to the sugar era of the island.

The hike starts with a drive to the parking, to get there, take the national road 9 which crosses the island towards Sainte-Anne at the bottom of the island. Before arriving at the village of Sainte-Anne follow the direction of Cap Chevalier for 1km. Turn right for 2km and follow the path but beware, this road has
several big rainwater channels, and crossing them can be a bit tricky if your car is low, let alone rental cars. Once you've conquered this, you are now good to go for the hike.

The Hike

From the car park, it takes around 40 minutes to hike all the way to the top, whereas the return is faster. Although it goes uphill significantly, the
path has been intelligently laid with stairs to make it accessible. It's most certainly for those who enjoy beautiful scenery. This trail is steep and for the most part made of stones and stairs, so it's not advised for people with bad

knees. However, the climb is easily manageable and well-indicated so that you will stay on the right path.

Once you reach the top, you get a 360-degree reward in breathtaking views that give value to this hike. The panorama is simply magnificent and offers an orientation table that identifies landmarks. This beautiful viewpoint is ideal for taking pictures and absorbing the natural beauty of Martinique.

This hike could last an average 1h30 depending on the individual, it is about 3km.

Photo by Jametlene Reskp (Unsplash)

Tips for Hikers

> **Families:** The hike is fairly simple but has high steps, which might be challenging for young children. Some hikers have taken an hour to reach the top with young kids, showing that it's possible with patience and a bit of effort.

Fitness Level: While it's a short hike, it can get your heart pumping, making it a good little cardio workout.

What to See: Down near the parking lot, you'll find the ruins of a sugar house, though you cannot visit as it's fenced off. The hike itself winds through a beautiful forest, adding to the charm and variety of the experience.

Culinary – Where to Eat

When visiting Sainte-Anne, there are several noteworthy dining options to consider, each offering a unique culinary experience. Here are some of the top places to eat, along with their cuisine types and price ranges..

Delim's

Specializing in French cuisine, Delim's offers a high-end dining experience, making it a refreshing change from typical Caribbean tourist food.

Prices range: $$ - $$$$.

People Beach

This restaurant serves a mix of French and Caribbean dishes.

Price range: $$ - $$$.

Le Man-Soufran

Offering both French and Caribbean cuisine, Le Man-Soufran is praised for its excellent atmosphere, delicious food, and top-notch service

Price range: $$ - $$$.

Chez Olivier

An excellent spot for lunch, Chez Olivier specializes in Caribbean cuisine made from fresh ingredients. It's perfect for a healthy meal in a relaxed setting, and it's budget-friendly.

Price range: $.

Chez Syssy

Located few blocks from the Salines Beach (Plage des Salines), this restaurant serves French and Caribbean food.

Price range $$ - $$$.

Oasis Italia

For pizza lovers, Oasis Italia is a must-visit. This Italian restaurant offers a variety of pizzas and is great for a family evening out.

Price range: $$ - $$$.

Ti Cozy

Offering delightful French cuisines with a menu that combines the best of Martinique and Brittany.

Price Range: $

Le Cocotier

Located on the beach, Le Cocotier is known for its fresh and delicious Caribbean cuisine.

Price Range: $

Restaurant SNACK BOUBOU BOKITS - depuis 2006

Famous for its BOKITS sandwiches, this restaurant offers a slow dining experience to savor every bite.

Price Range: $

La Cour Creole

Offering Caribbean cuisines, this restaurant is known for its friendly staff, good chicken, pork, and shrimp dishes, and a selection of good wine.

Price Range: $$ - $$$

Resto Madinina Breizh

A top fish restaurant with an authentic and excellent menu. They also serve French and Caribbean cuisines.

Price Range: $$ - $$$

For more restaurants in Sainte Anne.... **Scan code**

Accommodation – Where to Stay

The charming town of Sainte Anne offers a range of accommodations that cater to different tastes and budgets. Whether you're looking for an all-inclusive resort or a cozy eco-friendly stay, Sainte-Anne has something for everyone. Here are some top places to consider:

Club Med Les Boucaniers - Martinique

Type: Resort (All-Inclusive)

This Caribbean resort with a strong French feel is great for French speakers. It provides a range of activities, entertainment, and watersports, all located in a lovely seaside location. This resort is ranked as the finest bargain in Sainte-Anne. Perfect for those wishing to experience a premium all-inclusive trip with spectacular ocean views and world-class restaurants.

La Dunette

Type: Hotel

La Dunette is noted for its handy location and inviting environment. Guests have liked their stays here, especially after lengthy flights. It's a perfect place for people wishing to unwind before traveling back home

Residence Orcea Ecofriendly

Type: Condominium

This eco-friendly property is nestled amid a verdant paradise and offers an exceptional experience with its outdoor ambiance.

Anoli Lodges Village

Type: Specialty Inn

Known for its lovely Creole houses built on a high hill with views of Le Marin bay. It is a popular among returning tourists to Martinique. The home also boasts a pool, making it a fantastic alternative for anyone wanting a tranquil and gorgeous visit

Le Hameau de Beauregard

Type: Apartments

This well-equipped and roomy hotel is near to the shopping and beach of Sainte-Anne. It's a terrific alternative for guests searching for a comfortable setting with all the services nearby.

For more hotels and booking options **scan code**

Itinerary

Day 1: Arrival and Relaxation

As you arrive at Martinique Aimé Césaire International Airport in Le Lamentin, a sense of excitement fills the air, heralding the beginning of your island adventure. After picking up your rental car, take a scenic drive south to Sainte-Anne, where lush landscapes and breathtaking coastal views accompany you on your journey. Once you reach your accommodation—be it the luxurious Club Med Les Boucaniers, the eco-friendly Residence Orcea, or the charming Anoli Lodges Village—unpack your bags and settle in, allowing the vibrant island vibes to wash over you.

After taking some time to relax, head to Chez Olivier for your first meal on the island. Here, you can indulge in delicious local Creole dishes, each bite serving as a tantalizing introduction to the culinary delights of Martinique. Post-lunch, make your way to La Pointe Marin, an idyllic beach boasting calm waters and shaded spots perfect for unwinding. Stretch out on the warm sand, dip your toes in the refreshing water, and let the relaxation truly begin.

As the sun begins to set, it's time to enjoy dinner at Le Cocotier. With a menu that offers a delightful blend of local and international flavors, you'll end your first day on a satisfying note. The ambiance is perfect for reflecting on the beautiful start to your journey in Martinique, setting the stage for the adventures yet to come.

Day 2: Beach Day at Plage des Salines

Start your day early at Plage des Salines, one of Martinique's most renowned beaches, where arriving ahead of the crowds guarantees you a prime spot on the soft, white sands. Spend the morning swimming and sunbathing while soaking up the serene atmosphere; for added comfort, consider renting a deckchair to let the gentle waves rock you into relaxation. When lunchtime rolls around, treat yourself to delectable Creole specialties from one of the beachside restaurants, complemented perfectly by refreshing coconut water and delightful ice cream. Afterward, take a leisurely stroll along the expansive beach, marveling at the stunning scenery and enjoying the tranquil environment all around you. As the day winds down, head to Chez Syssy for dinner, a place celebrated for its warm ambiance and delicious local cuisine, where you can savor the rich flavors of Martinique and unwind after a blissful day.

Day 3: Hiking Adventure at Savane des Pétrifications

Start your day with an adventurous hike at Savane des Pétrifications, where the unique desert-like landscape offers a striking contrast to Martinique's lush greenery. As you explore, marvel at the fascinating rock formations and the colorful chalcedony scattered throughout the area. Be sure to wear sturdy shoes, bring plenty of water, and set off early to make the most of your adventure while avoiding the heat. After your hike, you can either enjoy a packed picnic or find a cozy spot at a nearby restaurant to refuel. Once you've replenished your energy, head back to your accommodation for some well-deserved rest. In the evening, make your way to La Cour Creole for dinner, where you can soak in the vibrant atmosphere and savor the flavorful dishes that showcase the rich culinary traditions of the island.

Day 4: Exploring Etang des Salines and Anse Michel

Start your day with a peaceful walk along the boardwalk at Etang des Salines, where the serene environment and vibrant flora and fauna create a perfect backdrop for morning reflections. After your stroll, take a scenic drive to Anse Michel, enjoying the beautiful path that winds through the mangroves leading to the beach. Once you arrive, grab a snack from a local vendor and relax on the beach as you watch kite surfers showcasing their skills or take a refreshing swim to the nearby islets. The calm waters and stunning surroundings provide an ideal setting for unwinding. As evening approaches, treat yourself to dinner at Resto Madinina Breizh, where the restaurant's creative blend of local ingredients and French culinary flair promises a delightful dining experience to end your day on a high note.

Day 5: Fun at Maya Beach Club and Anse Trabaud

Start your day with a blast at Maya Beach Club, where an exciting array of inflatable games and activities guarantees a morning full of fun for the whole family. Don't forget to put on life jackets and dive into the water! After enjoying the playful morning, take a break for a light meal at the nearby snack bar before heading off on an adventure to the more secluded Anse Trabaud. Be ready for a bumpy ride, and possibly a hike if the toll gate is closed, but the effort will be rewarded with the beauty of this pristine beach. As the day winds down, treat yourself to a delicious dinner at Oasis Italia, where the relaxed atmosphere is perfect for unwinding after a day packed with fun and exploration.

Day 6: Hiking Piton de Crêve Cœur and Exploring Sainte-Anne

In the morning, set off to the starting point of the Piton de Crêve Cœur hike, where a challenging climb awaits, offering stunning 360-degree views at the summit. As you explore the remnants of Habitation Crève-Cœur, be sure to capture plenty of photos of the breathtaking vistas. After the hike, enjoy a leisurely lunch at Ti Cozy, savoring delicious local specialties. The afternoon can be spent strolling through the vibrant town of Sainte-Anne, where you can visit local shops and soak up the lively atmosphere. As the day winds down, treat yourself to a satisfying dinner at Delim's, where the blend of local and international dishes promises to round off another perfect day on the island.

Day 7: Farewell to Sainte-Anne

As your time on the enchanting island of Martinique comes to a close, take a moment to bask in the sun at Pointe Marin or Anse Michel, allowing the warmth to envelop you as you reflect on the unforgettable experiences you've gathered. In the afternoon, return to your accommodation to pack up and prepare for departure. Treat yourself to a final meal at People Beach, where the stunning seaside views and delectable cuisine create the perfect backdrop for your last moments. With a heart brimming with cherished memories, make your way to Martinique Aimé Césaire International Airport, ready to bid a fond farewell to this beautiful paradise.

Saint-Pierre

Located on the Caribbean coast of Martinique, Sainte Pierre was once known as "Little Paris" due to its cultural and architectural grandeur. Its dramatic change came in 1902 with the eruption of Mount Pelée. But having grown from the ashes, the city welcomes its guests with a unique combination of historical intrigue and natural beauty.

The Story of Saint-Pierre

Sainte Pierre's history started in September 1635 when Pierre Belain d'Esnambuc and a hundred colonists established the first long-lasting colony on Martinique. It had grown to over 5,000 by the 1660s and continued to emerge as a large city during the 18th and 19th centuries. It became a bustling commercial center, as vessels from everywhere in the world flocked to it, and boasted of a rich cultural life besides modern amenities like a cathedral, theater, running water, electricity, and even a tramway.

All that changed on May 8, 1902, when Mount Pelée had a disastrous eruption. In just 90 seconds, the city lay in ruin, with only two of its inhabitants out of 30,000 surviving, including prisoner Cyparis, who survived due to the thickness of his dungeon's walls. The eruption also razed about 40 ships anchored in the bay; only the Roddam escaped the clouds of fire. A sad turning point in the story of Sainte Pierre indeed, and Fort-de-France took over as the commercial capital.

Rebirth and Rediscovery

It was not until the 1920s that Sainte Pierre really began to regain its structure. Today, this is a charming town of some 4,500 residents, labeled the 101st "City of Art and History" in 1990. The attractiveness of the town lies in the merger of ancient ruins with a very lively local culture.

Photo by Cynthia Cadoni (unsplash)

Getting There

It is by no means difficult to reach Sainte Pierre. The nearest airport, Aimé Césaire International Airport, lies 25 km away from the commune. Car rentals and taxis are readily available to Sainte Pierre from this airport. If the sea route were to be considered, then the anchorage facility of the yachts and cruise ships at the Port of Fort-de-France, lying 31 kilometers away from Sainte Pierre, is good. When you travel to Sainte Pierre, you should have with you a valid identity document or passport. Just like for any travel, there isn't any particular vaccination required, but you are strongly advised to have universal vaccinations.

Navigating Around Sainte Pierre

Once in Sainte Pierre, transportation is fairly simple. The city is small and can be readily seen on foot. If you want to take a better look around the city, take a small train ride that offers guided tours across the city. It's a great way to discover the rich history and all the major attractions within a short period of time.

Tourist Attraction

Mount Pelée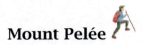

Volcano, hike spot

 [Saint-Pierre 97250, Martinique](#)

Journeying to the summit of Montagne Pelée in Martinique offers an unforgettable adventure for those seeking both a physical challenge and stunning views. Although there are several trails to hike Mount Pelée, popular trail you could follow is the **"Aileron trail"** The trek begins with a scenic drive to the Aileron parking lot, where hikers should start around noon when the weather is cooler and less windy.

The Hike (Aileron trail)

Starting Point: L'Aileron Parking Lot Most hikers begin their ascent from the Aileron parking lot. It's advisable to start your hike around noon when the weather tends to be cooler and less windy. The initial part of the hike involves a climb up poorly maintained stairs, where you'll likely encounter many other hikers.

First Section: Steep Climb

The first part of the trail goes uphill in a steep climb along the mountain's side. This part of the hike represents the most strenuous and requires a good level of physical fitness. Make sure to wear sturdy hiking boots and bring plenty of water and snacks.

Second Part: The Crater Rim

After the initial ascent, it would take one up to the top into an area called the Caldeira, a ridge walk around the top of the crater. Spectacular views from this half of the hike show Martinique's north and west sides, towards the Caribbean Sea, and down into the crater itself. Sceneries here are simply breathtaking, with the lush green vegetation and flowers yellow and red adding a splash of color to the landscape.

Third Section: Le Chinois Spur Trail or Ascent to the Chinese

The final ascent to the peak is along the Le Chinois spur trail, a tricky path strewn with large, sharp boulders. This part of the hike is the most challenging but also the most rewarding. On clear days, you'll be treated to panoramic views of Martinique, the Caribbean Sea, and even Saint Lucia in the distance.

Descent: The Ravine

The descent takes you through a deep ravine, where you'll need to scramble down wet, rocky trails using both hands and feet. After crossing the ravine, you'll climb a series of steps and ladders to ascend the hillside on the other side. The return trip offers different perspectives and stunning views, especially if the weather has cleared up.

This hike offers a mix of breathtaking views and lush vegetation, so it's essential to bring water and snacks due to the intense effort required for both the ascent and descent. Weather can be unpredictable, with clouds and rain sometimes obscuring the view, so choose a clear day for your hike. If it's hot, start early to avoid the midday heat.

Tips for Hikers

- **Footwear:** Wear welly boots or hiking boots due to the river of water running down parts of the trail.

- **Physical Condition:** This hike is physically demanding and not recommended for novice hikers. Ensure you are in good shape before attempting the climb.

- **Timing:** The entire hike can take about 4 and half hours or even more depending on your pace, allowing for a leisurely pace to enjoy the surroundings and take breaks.

- **Come ready**: There's a restaurant and facilities at the bottom, but on the hike, it's you and the mountain. Sturdy shoes are a must (it gets slippery), bring layers because the weather changes fast, and also bring a headlamp just incase you are caught up in the dark.

Distillerie Depaz

Rum distillery

 [_Plantation de la Montagne Pelée, Saint-Pierre 97250, Martinique_](#)

Entrance fee: free

Tucked down at the foot of Mount Pelée in the lush surroundings, Distillerie Depaz is a little treasure in Martinique. Operating with an old steam engine running the mills to crush sugar cane and the columns to distill rum, this little distillery stays faithful to its beginnings.

Distillery Depaz's past is as rich and multifarious as its rums. Victor Depaz started the distillery at Mount Pelée's base in 1917 following the disastrous eruption there in 1902. He had also created a stunning château on the grounds by 1922. The distillery keeps expanding today, handling its own sugar cane, fermenting, distilling, and maturing a wide spectrum of fine rums.

Photo by Kathleen jarchow (unsplash)

As a tourist, you can tour the immaculate gardens and view the amazing machinery engaged in the rum-making process. The experience is magically enhanced by the graceful château and the background of the rising volcano. Though queues for samples might be long, the store has a large assortment of rums, many of which are difficult to locate elsewhere. For a more informative visit, it's advisable to book extra time for an audio-guided tour.

Many people rave about the distillery's outstanding rums and picturesque surroundings and all this makes it a worthy stop. It's worth mentioning that while the distillery itself allows free visitation, there is a small price of around **5 -7 euros** to tour the château and for tastings. You could also purchase vintage rums at the shop although they are a bit pricey than the ones outside.

Mémorial De La Catastrophe De 1902

Museum

 169 D10, Saint-Pierre 97250, Martinique

Opening hour: 9am – 6pm

Entrance fee: €8

While in Sainte Pierre, take the time to visit the Mémorial De La Catastrophe De 1902, or as it is more commonly known, the

Frank A. Perret Museum. For such a small museum, it is rather longwinded on the eruption of Mount Pelée that destroyed the town in 1902. The museum, set in the heart of Saint-Pierre, was for the memory of those who have died and survived the disaster. Although some visitors feel that the museum could be larger, it does an exceptional job detailing the catastrophic event. The well-curated exhibits and the interesting audio guide-which are available in both English and French revives the history of this particular disaster in Saint-Pierre.

One thing to consider is that sometimes the welcome to the museum may be a bit lacking, and you may find yourself going through the exhibits in about 35 or 40 minutes. Despite this, the entrance fee of €8 is fair for the wealth of information provided. The museum provides a powerful account of the eruption in great detail, with the names of most of the victims inscribed on its walls. If you are traveling to Saint-Pierre, it is essential for any tourist to visit this location, as it provides a deeper understanding of that significant event in Martinique's history, which is likely to leave a lasting impression on their mind.

Tip

For an enriching historical experience, use the audio guide to fully immerse yourself in the story. If you visit in September, you're likely to enjoy a quieter, more personal tour. All in all, while the museum has its quirks, it's a poignant and informative stop that truly enhances any visit to Sainte-Pierre.

Cachot de Cyparis

Historical landmark

[PRWF+VMQ, Ruelle Labadie, Saint-Pierre 97250, Martinique](#)

Entrance fee: free

The Cachot de Cyparis is an absolute must-see when one visits Saint-Pierre. Infamous and more known as a dungeon, it holds an interesting story about a certain Louis-Auguste Cyparis, who survived the ravaging eruption of Mount Pelée on May 8, 1902, with only a few burns, while the rest of the city got tragically destroyed. His survival is an intriguing story of destiny and grit. But the Cachot de Cyparis is more than a very important historical object; entry to the site is also free, thus rendering it an accessible and enriching part of your visit. You can't help but reflect on the quite astonishing good fortune of Cyparis and the incredible strength of nature as you make your way around what is left of the dungeon.

This is an interesting site for families, as children will surely be fascinated by the story of Monsieur Cyparis. It is interesting from an educational perspective, both for kids and history enthusiasts. While in Saint-Pierre, couple this visit with a tour around the ruins of the nearby theater and the memorial. At several places on the site, information panels give a good overview of the aspects of the city before the eruption. This trio of sites really creates a vivid picture of times gone by and is an enoteca-like experience that serves to underline the impermanence of life. In other words, the Cachot de Cyparis is not some kind of tourist trap but a symbol of human survival during the disaster—a true reminder that should not be missed when venturing to Saint-Pierre.

Photo by Jorgen Hendriksen (unsplash)

A Papa D'Lo Plongée

Diving spot

 [104 D10, Saint-Pierre 97250, Martinique](#)

Bienvenue à A Papa D'Lo Plongée, this is your ticket to an unforgettable diving adventure in Saint-Pierr. With its scenic oceanfront location, this dive club offers deep and technical dives and thus stands out among the crowd for divers of every level.

Unparalleled Diving Experience

The A Papa D'Lo Plongée training sessions are well-organized, safely run, and manage to mix learning with adventure. Be it a novice to take a first plunge or a seasoned diver who enjoys deep dives on shipwrecks, this club have something that suits everyone's interest. The dive sites, including the impressive Roraima wreck, are only a 20-minute sail away. It promises you get some of the most stunning underwater sites in such a short time.

The dive shop itself is large and well-organized, with a big change room, a rinsing room, and showers. The boat is one built for 30 divers, but very nicely laid out, with intelligent touches such as square-cross-section ladder bars to make fin boarding so much easier and ample room for tanks.

The team working in A Papa D'Lo Plongée is described as professional and friendly. Sure, they work in French, but some of them speak English too, and though it may be a problem, they will do their best to make things go as easily and pleasantly as possible. After your dive, you can unwind at the club's sea-view terrace with a free drink or even attend a theory lesson. The place is very popular both among locals and tourists for its friendly atmosphere and professionalism.

A Papa D'Lo Plongée prides itself on being respectful of the environment; it makes sure your diving adventure is both thrilling and sustainable.

Whether it be the diving spots, professional team full of friendliness, or well-organized structure, well, A Papa D'Lo Plongée promises a diving experience which will make you want to return.

Eglise du Fort

Historical landmark

 26 D10A, Saint-Pierre 97250, Martinique

Nestled in the historic "Fort" neighborhood of Sainte Pierre, the Eglise du Fort is a poignant reminder of the city's sad past and its unconquerable spirit. The ruins of this once grand church, razed to the ground by the destructive eruption of Mount Pelée in 1902, give a hauntingly fascinating look at nature's violence and the frailty of man's creations.

The visit to Eglise du Fort is a journey down the lanes of time. The ruins stand in stark testimony to that cloud of fire that swept through the city, thereby leaving the church with pieces of walls and an overturned bell tower. It is a site carrying its peculiar charm amidst ruins; big chunks of the building are intact, silently standing as witnessing fixtures for the past.

A tour of this place might be short, usually half an hour or more, making it an ideal stop among the other historical sites of Sainte Pierre. You will notice informative panels with the texts given both in French and in English, which give a crystal-clear overview of what this church used to be like before the eruption, and it helps to enhance your imagination regarding what it once looked like in its glory and what would become an event that changed everything.

The Fort Neighborhood

The "Fort" quarter is the oldest part of the town that has taken the brunt of the eruption fury. You could feel the mark left by the burning cloud while walking past this area; in some places, the grass grew over, adding to the eerie beauty of the ruins. Although less maintained than other sites like the theater, the church remains deeply moving, evoking a sense of solemn reflection.

Although most of the church has been destroyed, you can still tell where the altars, side chapels, and the latter now standing independently from the rest of the structure- were situated. There's more in the small museum next door, which preserves statues that are in better condition, including an impressive marble lamb and the half-melted bronze bell.

Though it may not be as widely known as Pompeii, Eglise du Fort does have an odd sort of magic. The site itself-a natural setting in which life goes on around contributes in no small way to such mystique. The actual ruins, burnt cement, the fallen columns, and the melted marble continue to echo today, a very strong reminder of what happened in 1902 and the resilience that still works in Sainte Pierre.

Accommodation – Where to Stay

For hotels and places to stay at Sainte Pierre check

TripAdvisor

Where to Eat - Restaurants

Restaurant Bar Le Reservoir 1902

> **Cuisine: Caribbean**
>
> **Price Range: $$ - $$$**
>
> **Highlights:** This restaurant offers a magnificent view of the bay of Saint-Pierre. The cuisine is delicious, and the service is efficient.

2. Le Mix

> **Cuisine: French, Cafe**
>
> **Price Range: $$ - $$$**
>
> **Highlights:** Le Mix is known for its calm ambiance, making it a perfect spot to relax and enjoy a sunset. The location is ideal for a quiet moment of relaxation in Sainte Pierre.

3. Le Maxximum

> **Cuisine: French, Caribbean**

Price Range: $$ - $$$

Highlights: This place offers a typical Martinican dining experience.

4. Le VSP

Cuisine: French, Caribbean

Highlights: A pleasant spot for lunch with well-presented dishes served quickly. The warm welcome and the view facing the sea add to the delightful dining experience.

5. Arhum Glacé

Cuisine: Fast Food, Street Food

Price Range: $$ - $$$

Highlights: Renowned for having the best ice cream in Martinique, Arhum Glacé is a must-visit for ice cream lovers. Their homemade ice cream is highly recommended.

6. Chez Marie-Claire

Highlights: A lively spot offering good value meals. The dish "Macadam" is simple but delightful, featuring rice and fish. The vibrant atmosphere makes it a fun place to dine.

7. Bela Beach

Cuisine: Bars & Pubs, French

Price Range: $$ - $$$

Highlights: known for its delicious food and great service in a beautiful setting. The fricassée de chatrou is a standout dish.

8. La Vague

Cuisine: Caribbean

Price Range: $$ - $$$

Highlights: A good spot for lunch, offering dishes like choucroute de la mer. The view from the restaurant enhances the dining experience.

9. L'Alsace a Kay

Cuisine: French, European

Price Range: $$ - $$$

Highlights: Perfect for Sunday lunch, with specials like chicken cooked in a clay pot. The atmosphere is cozy and inviting.

10. Kaï Raymond

Cuisine: French, Caribbean

Price Range: $$ - $$$

Highlights: Known for its amazing fruit juices and delicious food. The assiette d'accras is a must-try.

11. Le Fromager

Cuisine: Caribbean

Price Range: $$ - $$$

Highlights: Offers a unique self-serve aperitif bar experience with good food and a great view. The interesting concept adds to the charm of this restaurant.

12. Le Moulin A Cannes

Cuisine: Caribbean

Price Range: $$ - $$$

Highlights: Known for its excellent food and incredible views. The gastronomic delights make it a must-visit, although it closes soon.

For more restaurants check here..

Itinerary

5-Day Itinerary for Sainte Pierre, Martinique

Day 1: Arrival and Introduction to Sainte Pierre

Your journey begins at Aimé Césaire International Airport, just a short 25 km drive from Sainte Pierre. After collecting your rental car or hopping in a taxi, you'll be on your way to this historic gem. Once you arrive and settle into your accommodation, take a leisurely stroll around the town to get your bearings. Sainte Pierre, with its compact size, is perfect for exploring on foot. Make your first stop the Mémorial De La Catastrophe De 1902. This small but poignant museum provides a detailed account of the catastrophic eruption of Mount Pelée in 1902, which decimated the town. The exhibits and audio guide bring to life the tragic history of Sainte Pierre, offering a moving introduction to the area. After the museum, wander through the nearby ruins of the town's theater and the Cachot de Cyparis, where you can learn about the incredible survival story of Louis-Auguste Cyparis. In the evening, enjoy a delightful dinner at Restaurant Bar Le Reservoir 1902, sampling Caribbean cuisine while reflecting on the day's discoveries.

Day 2: Exploring Nature and History

Rise early for a hearty breakfast before embarking on an adventure to Mount Pelée. The Aileron trail is a popular route for hiking up this iconic volcano. Starting from the L'Aileron parking lot around noon when the weather is cooler, the hike takes you through lush vegetation, steep climbs, and breathtaking views. As you ascend, you'll be rewarded with panoramic vistas of Martinique and the Caribbean Sea. The final ascent to the peak, though challenging, is immensely rewarding, offering a sense of accomplishment and awe. After descending, head to Distillerie Depaz at the foot of the mountain. This charming distillery, with its old steam engine and stunning château, offers an insightful tour of the rum-making process. Sample some of the finest rums and soak in the beautiful surroundings. For dinner, consider dining at Le Mix, where you can enjoy French cuisine in a cozy, cafe-style setting.

Day 3: Diving into Marine Wonders

Today is all about the ocean. Start your morning at A Papa D'Lo Plongée, a highly recommended dive club. Whether you're a novice or an experienced diver, this club offers a range of dives to suit all levels. Explore the stunning underwater world, including the impressive Roraima wreck. The friendly and professional team ensures a safe and enjoyable experience. After a morning of diving, relax at the club's sea-view terrace with a refreshing drink. In the afternoon, explore more of Sainte Pierre's maritime history with a visit to the Eglise du Fort. The ruins of this church, destroyed in the 1902 eruption, provide a hauntingly beautiful glimpse into the past. Informative panels help you imagine what the church once looked like before nature's fury. For dinner, try Le Maxximum, where you can enjoy a blend of French and Caribbean dishes.

Day 4: Cultural and Historical Immersion

Spend your fourth day delving deeper into the cultural and historical fabric of Sainte Pierre. Start with a visit to the town's bustling market, where you can sample local produce and interact with friendly vendors. Then, make your way to the Cachot de Cyparis, revisiting the story of Louis-Auguste Cyparis and contemplating his incredible survival. For lunch, head to Le VSP, a restaurant known for its delicious French-Caribbean fusion cuisine. In the afternoon, visit the Musée Volcanologique Franck Perret, another excellent museum dedicated to the 1902 eruption. The exhibits here are comprehensive and fascinating, offering a deeper understanding of the disaster. Spend the evening at Arhum Glacé, a casual spot perfect for street food and a relaxed atmosphere.

Day 5: Leisure and Farewell

On your final day, take it easy and enjoy the laid-back vibe of Sainte Pierre. Start with a leisurely breakfast at Chez Marie-Claire, known for its friendly service and delicious offerings. Afterward, visit the picturesque ruins of the Fort quarter, where you can wander among the remnants of the town's oldest neighborhood. The combination of historical intrigue and natural beauty makes for a reflective morning. In the afternoon, if you feel like another dip in the ocean, head back to A Papa D'Lo Plongée for a final dive or simply relax on the beach. For your last dinner in Sainte Pierre, treat yourself to a meal at Le Fromager, where you can savor exquisite Caribbean flavors while enjoying a view of the setting sun. As you prepare to leave this enchanting town, take with you the memories of its rich history, natural beauty, and the warm hospitality of its people.

Trois-Ilets

Trois-Ilets, located just barely across the bay from Martinique's dynamic capital, Fort-de-France, is a beautiful combination of natural beauty and cultural depth. This gorgeous town on the southwestern coast is known for its sandy beaches, lush tropical surroundings, and intriguing blend of historical and modern attractions.

Getting there

Getting to Trois-Ilets is easy and straightforward. It is regularly served by ferryboats from Fort-de-France. You can take one at Anse Mitan, Pointe du Bout, or Anse à l'Ane each offering unique entrance to this area. The ferry ride itself is a pleasure, as you can gaze at the beautiful sight of the bay and get tanned under the Caribbean sun.

Navigating Around Trois Ilet

Once you arrive, navigating about Trois-Ilets is simple. Taxis are frequently accessible and provide a convenient choice for exploring locations beyond walking distance. For those who prefer a slower pace, the town's modest size makes it ideal for wandering. You'll find picturesque streets lined with shops, cafés, and restaurants, all conveniently located near major hotels and resorts.

Trois-Ilets is considered Martinique's premier resort town, which has managed to combine an abundance of tourist-friendly amenities with a good dose of authentic local charm.

It works as a great home base for visitors who want to explore the island during the day and party hard at night. Be it luxurious resorts or cozy boutique hotels, comfortable accommodation is available to cater to every traveler's taste.

Among the major sights of interest in Trois-Ilets, there is rich cultural heritage. The town contains numerous historic places: famous La Pagerie Museum, the childhood home of Empress Joséphine; intriguing Village de la Poterie, where one can get the course of making traditional pottery.

For the beach lovers, this is a spoil of choices, as beaches like Anse Mitan and Anse à l'Ane are excellent spots for swimming, sunbathing, and water sports. The waters are crystal clear, with excellent conditions for snorkeling among vibrant marine life.

Tourist Attraction

La Savane des Esclaves

History Museum

 La Ferme, Les Trois-Îlets 97229, Martinique

Opening Hours: 9:00 am - 4:30 pm

Tour duration: About 1 – 2 hours

The Savane des Esclaves is a rare treasure only minutes from the main town of Trois Islet in Martinique. Created by Gilbert

Larose, an impassioned historian, this private site takes visitors through 400 years of Martinique's history-from the pre-European Amerindian era, through the harrowing period of slavery, to the rural way of life post-abolition up until the 1960s. It is not an exhibit of history, but rather an engrossing educational experience nestled within a beautiful, well-cared-for garden area.

Visitors can explore the property at their own pace, guided by informational signs, both in English and French. These informational displays, along with a video that includes an English subtitle feature, make the complicated history and personal tales of the island's past available to one and all. A video, narrated by Larose himself, eliminates the need for guided tours and orients guests before they take their own self-guided tour.

Photo by SweetMellowChill (Pixabay)

As you walk through the exhibits, the narrative vividly brings to life the struggles and resilience of the enslaved people. The beautiful gardens are serene yet poignantly contrasting with the somber history depicted here. The attention to detail in the displays offers visitors a sense of the weight of oppression and the triumphs of those who endured it. This open-air museum is a memorial, dedicated to the strength and spirit of those who had to endure during those dark times, and hence it is an emotionally touching experience. The facility is spotless and well thought out for an enriching visit. Comfortable walking shoes are advisable as there are some steep walkways and steps, and a trekking pole may be useful if needed. While the historical content can be quite challenging, the site is also suitable for families. Children can learn about this important part of history in an engaging yet educating manner, even though the tour is quite short.

The Savane des Esclaves is more than just a museum; it invites reflection and learning, resulting in a tranquil place with rich flora. Then there is the addition of the new café offering refreshments—including these very tasty juices made from farm-fresh fruits—and a shop featuring local products and books. For our recommendation, La Savane des Esclaves should be on the bucket list for anyone traveling to Martinique in search of learning more about Martinique and the history of the Caribbean. It is a place reaching to the heart and soul, enabling all visitors to enjoy an even deeper understanding and appreciation of what it truly means to be Martinican. This educational outing is not only informative but also a beautiful and serene experience, making it one of the most compelling historical sites in the Caribbean.

Musee de la Pagerie - *History of Empress Josephine*

Speciality Museums

 [D38, Les Trois-Îlets 97229, Martinique](#)

Opening hours: 9:00 AM - 4:00 PM

Tour duration 1-2 hours

Entrance fee: Adults: €4 (except 65 years or older: €2)

Students: €1

People with disability: €2

Tucked down in the center of Martinique, the Musée de la Pagerie is an intriguing place that vividly brings history to life. Set on the ancient farm where Napoleon Bonaparte's wife, Empress Josephine, spent her infancy, this magical museum gives guests a great window into the French past and the complicated legacy of colonization.

Getting here from Fort de France

To go to the museum, leave Fort-de-France via the A1 motorway and continue on the island with the N5. Two roundabouts are passed at Ducos, the zone of activities, then two at Rivière-Salée. After the last roundabout, take a right on D7 in the direction of Trois-Îlets. After 10 minutes, you will get to the Cartel of Mangofil, Alfareros Pueblo, and just before it, the Museum of Caña de Azúcar. Continue toward Pointe du Bout until you reach Pueblo de Trois-

Îlets. Pueblo Ataviese is in the same direction as Pointe du Bout and is literally in the middle of the golf course area of the city. The Busque Cartel is the same as the Museo Pagerie. Head toward the city on the D38 and position yourself in front of the Museo de la Pagerie, simple to distinguish because there are ruins of an ancient factory next to it.

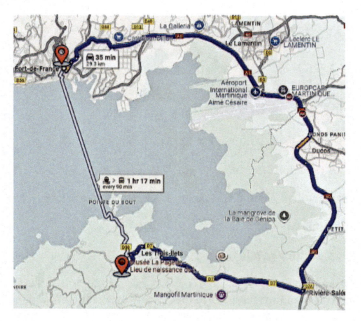

Guided tours, led by knowledgeable guides who seamlessly switch between French and English, provide fascinating insights into Josephine de Beauharnais' life and the historical context of the era. Although the main house no longer stands, the site includes several buildings such as a restored mill, the kitchen, and the remnants of a sugar factory. The museum also houses various artifacts related to Josephine and her time.

The grounds are beautifully scenic, making it a delightful place to wander and enjoy the natural surroundings, including a charming garden with occasional hummingbird sightings. The museum excels in contextualizing Josephine's life within the broader history of slavery and plantation labor in Martinique, with exhibits that are both informative and accessible. A visit typically takes about 1-2 hours, which is ample time to explore the exhibits and soak in the atmosphere. While the museum offers basic amenities like toilets, it lacks a café or restaurant, so bringing a picnic is advisable.

Visitor Tips

- **Language**: Most of the information is in French, but the staff are very helpful and can provide thorough tours in English.

- **Accessibility**: The site is fairly accessible for those with children or strollers, making it a convenient visit for families.

- **Preservation Efforts**: Entrance fees are quite low, especially for seniors, but the museum could benefit from additional funding to help preserve this important piece of history.

Anse Mitan

Beach

 Martinique

The picturesque Anse Mitan in Martinique is easily reached by a pleasant ferry ride. From the cruise terminal, the departure point for the ferries, it's an easy 20-minute, very pleasant stroll, and ticket buying is very straightforward. The ferry ride itself is a charming 25-minute journey to a small pier right onto the beach. Anse Mitan Beach is about a medium-sized beach that still retains much of its underdevelopment; this does carry with it a sense of calmness and relaxation. This is an ideal place to get some peace of mind, in addition to enjoying cozy bars and restaurants set throughout the shore. Be it a leisurely drink or a delicious meal you crave, there's ample opportunity to enjoy either one. The vibe here is relaxed, totally low key, making it so easy to just chill out.

The waters of Anse Mitan are crystal clear, making it a fantastic place for swimming and exploring marine life. Free showers and toilets on the beach add to the convenience, ensuring a comfortable visit. Because it is a popular tourist spot, the beach can get crowded, especially during peak times, so plan accordingly if you prefer a quieter experience.

One of the highlights of visiting Anse Mitan is the stunning views. Climbing to the heights offers breathtaking vistas of the bay of Fort-de-France. Even from the beach, you can enjoy spectacular sunsets that paint the sky in vibrant hues at the end of the day.

For those seeking a bit of adventure, there are areas along the beach that offer activities like jet skiing and towed buoys. These activities add an element of fun and excitement to your visit, making Anse Mitan a versatile destination that caters to both relaxation and adventure seekers.

Anse à l'Ane

Beach

 Martinique

Anse à l'Ane is a charming beach destination in Martinique, perfect for a relaxing day by the sea. It is easily reached by a local ferry, which offers a pictorial journey from Fort-de-France. The ferry ride itself is enjoyable, with stunning views of the bay before you reach the soft, sandy beach at Anse à l'Ane.

Once you get here, you find a beach with clear water, with plenty of shade due to the large number of palm and coconut trees bordering this beach. It is also an excellent destination for families, as the waters are peaceful and free from surf, hence very safe for kids while swimming or playing. You will also find restaurants, restrooms, or several bars to make your visit well-endowed. Lunchtime at Anse à l'Ane is a real treat, with a number of restaurants right on the beach offering everything from light snacks to gourmet cuisine, but at reasonable prices. Whether it's fresh seafood or just a snack you want, there's something to tempt your taste buds. The beach is friendly, with plenty of spots to lounge around in the shade provided either by the palm trees or by parasols available.

For those interested in exploring further, a water taxi service operates every 30-40 minutes, providing a quick and scenic link back to Fort-de-France. This allows you to enjoy the beach for a few hours or the entire day without any transportation concerns. Despite its popularity, Anse à l'Ane maintains a tranquil charm, especially on weekdays when the crowds are smaller. It's a family-friendly beach with a relaxed vibe, making it ideal for those looking to escape the busier tourist spots. The clear, calm waters are perfect for swimming and snorkeling, and the views across the bay to Fort-de-France are breathtaking.

Accommodations – where to stay

If you're looking for stylish accommodations in the bustling town of Trois-Ilets, consider the luxurious and relaxing Carayou Hotel & Spa. This hotel offers stunning views, a tranquil spa, and easy access to the beach, making it a perfect place to unwind after a day of exploration. Another excellent option is the Village Creole, which strikes a perfect balance between modern amenities and rustic charm. Nestled among charming boutiques and restaurants, it provides a taste of authentic Martinique life. With its vibrant atmosphere and quality services, the friendly hotel staff serves delicious food in an inviting setting, complemented by two enticing outdoor pools.

Lastly, Hotel La Pagerie boasts beautiful gardens and a modern design, providing a blissful retreat in the heart of Trois-Ilets. Each of these accommodations promises a delightful stay tailored to various tastes, ensuring a memorable trip for all visitors.

To look up more accommodations or for bookings **scan here**

Itinerary

5-day adventure itinerary to get the best of Trois Ilets

Day 1: Arrival and Introduction to Trois-Ilets

Your journey to Trois-Ilets begins with a scenic ferry ride from Fort-de-France, offering a delightful introduction to the beautiful bay. Choose from the ferry stops at Anse Mitan, Pointe du Bout, or Anse à l'Ane, each providing a unique entry into this charming town. The ferry ride itself is an experience, allowing you to soak in the Caribbean sun and stunning views.

Upon arrival, take a leisurely stroll through the town. Explore the quaint streets lined with shops, cafés, and restaurants. For lunch, savor some local Creole cuisine at one of the many eateries. Spend the afternoon unwinding at Anse Mitan Beach. Its clear waters and relaxed vibe make it the perfect spot for a swim or just lounging under the sun. In the evening, treat yourself to a seaside dinner while watching the sunset paint the sky in vibrant hues.

Day 2: Dive into History

Start your day with a visit to La Savane des Esclaves. This open-air museum, created by historian Gilbert Larose, offers a profound journey through Martinique's history. Wander through the beautiful gardens and informative exhibits at your own pace. The site's serene beauty juxtaposed with its somber history provides a deeply moving experience.

After a morning of reflection, head to the Musée de la Pagerie, the birthplace of Empress Josephine. A guided tour will take you through the remnants of the sugar plantation, offering insights into her life and the broader context of colonial Martinique. The lush gardens and historical artifacts make this a fascinating stop.

Day 3: Beach and Adventure

Today, venture to Anse à l'Ane Beach. The ferry ride to this tranquil spot is a visual treat, with stunning views of the bay. Spend your morning swimming in the calm, clear waters or relaxing under the shade of palm trees. For lunch, enjoy fresh seafood at one of the beachfront restaurants, savoring the laid-back atmosphere.

In the afternoon, add a bit of adventure to your day with some water sports. Try jet skiing or take a ride on a towed buoy for a thrilling experience. Alternatively, you can explore the marine life by snorkeling in the crystal-clear waters.

Day 4: Cultural Exploration and Shopping

Begin your day with a visit to the local markets in Trois-Ilets. Browse through stalls filled with colorful fruits, spices, and handmade crafts. It's a great place to pick up souvenirs and get a taste of local life.

In the afternoon, visit the House of Sugar (La Maison de la Canne). This museum delves into the history of sugar production in Martinique, showcasing the island's economic history and its connection to the sugar industry. The exhibits are both informative and engaging, offering a different perspective on the island's past.

Day 5: Relaxation and Farewell

Spend your final day in Trois-Ilets at leisure. Return to your favorite beach, whether it's Anse Mitan or Anse à l'Ane, and enjoy a relaxing morning. Take a long walk, swim in the warm waters, or simply bask in the sun.

For lunch, indulge in a delicious meal at one of the local restaurants, perhaps trying a dish you haven't yet sampled. In the afternoon, take a final stroll through the town, savoring the sights and sounds one last time.

Before departing, visit a local café for a refreshing drink made from farm-fresh fruits. Reflect on your wonderful experiences in Trois-Ilets and plan your return to this enchanting part of Martinique.

Le Francois

Getting There

Welcome to Le François, a hidden château located just twenty minutes from Martinique's main airport. This charming town is conveniently situated only twenty minutes away from the nearest beaches to the north and south, making it an ideal starting point for exploring the island. The road network has seen significant improvements in recent years, allowing you to reach the capital, Fort-de-France, in under 30 minutes, even during peak hours. If you're heading north, you can enjoy lush forests, rich heritage, and beautiful beaches, all within an hour's drive.

How to Get Around

Getting around Le François is quite easy. The town boasts a well-developed road network, facilitating smooth travel throughout the region. While public transportation is available, renting a car is recommended for a more flexible experience, allowing you to explore at your own pace and make spontaneous stops along the way.

A Glimpse into the Past

With a total area of more than 53 square kilometers, Le Francois is the third-largest commune on the island. In the beginning, the inhospitable shore was avoided by the early French immigrants. It wasn't until 1694, when Father Labat established a parish in this area, that the region started to become occupied. In order to accurately portray the town's long and illustrious past, the town's new concrete constructions are artfully incorporated with its antique wooden buildings.

Even up until very recently, Le Francois was an important figure in the field of international diplomacy. This was the location of the summit that took place in 1991 following the Gulf War. President George W. Bush and President Francois Mitterrand of France were both present at the summit. It is highly recommended that you pay a visit to the historic Habitation Clément, which served as the location of this gathering. It was in the year 1887 when Homère Clément, a dignitary who also served as the mayor of Le Francois, purchased the estate, which encompasses a total area of 300 hectares. There are four wineries on the premises, and they are bordered by gorgeous mahogany fields. It is famous for its outstanding Clément Rum, which is aged in these vineyards.

Local Attractions

Basically rural, Le François is one huge sugarcane field and st retches of banana plantations. Its most salient feature, however, is the bay itself, shallow and protected by a coral reef. The pristine waters of the bay provide a heavenly experience at spots like "Fonds Blancs" and "La Baignoire de Joséphine." Originally a recreational pursuit for the white Creole settlers, known as the "békés," the activity of boating to the sandy shallows has evolved into a cherished tradition for both residents and tourists. To fully enjoy this adventure, it's recommended to arrive at the nautical center early in the day to book a fisherman for a trip to one of the nearby islets.

Must-See Places

Le François is the main town on Martinique's Atlantic coast, boasting a population of about 16,000. You can explore the classic West Indian cemetery, which features distinctive black-and-white tiles, or visit the marina located at the edge of town. The area is home to two of Martinique's finest hotels, Cap Est and Hotel Plein Soleil, as well as some of the island's most upscale residences. A visit to the renowned Habitation Clément museum and distillery is a must.

Snorkeling and Island Adventures

Le François is also known for its excellent snorkeling opportunities. Off the coast, you'll find the privately owned Ilets de l'Impératrice. According to local legend, these islands were a favored bathing spot for Empress Joséphine, who enjoyed relaxing in the shallow, white-sand basins known as les fonds blancs. Whether you choose to snorkel or simply soak up the sun on these islands, you'll feel like you've discovered a little corner of paradise.

Tourist Attractions
La Baignoire de Joséphine (Josephine Bath)

Body of water

 Martinique

Opening hours: 8:00 AM - 7:00 PM

Ah, La Baignoire de Joséphine! If you're heading to Martinique, this is one spot you simply cannot miss. Located in Le François, this iconic destination is a treasure trove of experiences, eagerly waiting to be explored. Picture shallow sandbanks surrounded by a serene reef, making the waters calm and perfect for relaxation – it's no wonder it's a favorite spot for both locals and tourists alike. Your journey will take you to several enchanting islets: **Thierry Islet**, known for its excellent snorkeling trail; **Oscar Islet**, ideal for picnicking with a cozy guesthouse to boot; and **Long Islet**, boasting beautiful white sandy bottoms perfect for a leisurely swim. Out here, expect a vibrant atmosphere with tour groups mingling, vendors serving delicious Creole food, and tropical drinks that keep the spirits high. Fresh fruits add to the refreshing vibe of this tropical paradise. A lot of tourists rave about the tour, noting the great food, lovely snorkeling spots, and informative trips to places like Ile Chancel 🌊.

The sea remains calm, warm, and clear, making it a perfect setting for a relaxing boat ride. The boats are well-spaced, and the food and drinks on board are top-notch. For a unique experience, try a tour with King Mongin, known for warm welcomes, excellent entertainment, and scrumptious food, with many West Indians joining, adding an authentic local flavor to the experience. Don't forget your diving goggles; the underwater world here is mesmerizing with various fish and sea cucumbers to spot.

King Mongin

If you speak French, engage with the guides and fellow passengers to learn fascinating insights about Martinique that you won't find in any guidebook. Savor a tipunch, a traditional Martinican cocktail, while soaking in the beauty of the Atlantic Ocean. La Baignoire de Joséphine offers a perfect blend of relaxation, adventure, and cultural immersion. So, pack your swimwear, grab your camera, and get ready for an unforgettable day at sea!

Les Fonds Blancs

Body of water

Opening hours: 8:00 AM - 10:00 PM

Entrance fee: free

The Fonds Blancs are a secret treasure in the Caribbean Sea, located on the idyllic coastline of Martinique. The Fonds Blancs are a large, shallow area of the Atlantic coast that is sheltered by coral reefs and lies between the cities of Le Robert and Le Vauclin. This one-square-kilometer region gives a distinctive view of the sea along the islets of Thierry, Oscar, Métrente, and Long. The white sand and coral debris form a beautiful marine oasis, encouraging relaxation and fantasies, with a maximum depth of two meters.

Imagine taking in the sun and the breathtaking surroundings as you stroll out into the blue sea, where the water only reaches your waist. Away from the crowds, this location is ideal for a day of peaceful leisure. Bring plenty of sunscreen, pack a picnic, and get ready for an amazing adventure. The Fonds Blancs are a must-visit for anybody wishing to experience Martinique's natural beauty since they provide a balance of excitement and tranquility.

Insider Tip: Schedule your tour for a weekday and try to leave early, around 9 am, to take full advantage of the peace and quiet. Because of the timing, you'll frequently have places like La Baignoire de Joséphine virtually to yourself before the bigger crowds show up. The intimate experience is enhanced by the small group tours that several tour operators, including Côte au Vent, provide. The pristine seas, ideal for snorkeling, will captivate you during your visit. On one of the islands, you can have a delicious lunch and possibly see iguanas lounging in the sun. Some trips even provide vegetarian or vegan meals if you have special dietary requirements. The undersea environment is brimming with marine life, so don't forget to pack your snorkeling equipment.

Côte au Vent

For both couples and families, the Fonds Blancs are an excellent getaway. This undiscovered jewel of Martinique offers an amazing experience whether your goal is to unwind beneath the palm palms, explore the reefs, or just take in the stunning scenery. Thus, take a seat, unwind, and allow the Fonds Blancs' enchantment to enchant your senses.

Habitation Clement

Historical site

 [*domaine de l'acajou, Le François 97240, Martinique*](#)

Opening Hours: 9:00 AM - 6:30 PM

Entrance fee: €10

The 160-hectare Habitation Clément, tucked away in southeast Martinique, is more than just a farm; it's a piece of history. Imagine a magnificent 1700s Creole home encircled by an infinite supply of banana and sugarcane crops. Since 1887, the Clément family has lived on this magnificent estate for almost a century. It was designated a historical monument in 1996 and is home to the island's most well-known rum distillery as well as a renowned center for contemporary art.

Beautiful park-like landscapes greet you as soon as you enter this expansive agricultural area. Before you reach the former rum distillery and warehouses, take a leisurely stroll over walkways adorned with sculptures and colorful tropical greenery. You may see vintage machinery and a small portion of a sugar cane train that previously transported cane from the fields, even though the distillery is no longer in operation. During your tour there are bilingual info signs that provide brief insights about the place, but be sure to download an audio guide for a richer experience.

The pathway from the distillery leads to the plantation house. Here, you can explore a sitting room and a dining room set with fine china and polished long dining tables, adorned with lovely tropical flower arrangements. The original owner's family portraits fill the corridor, including a photo of the momentous encounter between Bush and Mitterrand. The actual house tour lasts only five minutes, but it is charming.

The contemporary rum tasting room and gift shop is where the trip comes to an end. A wonderful rum and fruit concoction and two robust rum samples are available for a fair **10€ entrance fee**. Even though the tasting is short, it provides a good introduction to the well-known rum made here. Although there isn't any food for sale at the estate, you are welcome to bring your own picnic to the tables that are provided. Parking is sufficient and the restrooms are clean, and the trails are paved and simple to use.

To truly enjoy the splendor of the grounds and the artwork strewn across the estate, allow at least three hours. It's a perceptive, engaging visit that always makes you feel welcome. A wonderful experience is guaranteed by the flawless service, which includes that of the young trainees. Habitation Clément is a must-see jewel in Martinique, regardless of your interests in art, history, or rum.

Insider Tips

- **Parking Pro Tip:** Skip that first lot you see and drive further up the hill for the main one.
- **Bring Your Lunch:** There's no cafe, and those nearby aren't always open. Pack a picnic and make a day of it!
- **Shoe Smarts:** This place involves some walking. Comfy shoes and water are your friends, especially for navigating between the distillery, gardens, and art.
- **For Art Lovers**: The sculptures and exhibits are awesome, especially the Dale Chihuly glass pieces. Don't miss them!

Distillerie Rhum A1710

Distillery

 [Habitation Le Simon, Le François 97240, Martinique](#)

Opening hours : 9 :00am – 5 :00pm

Nestled in the heart of the Caribbean, discover the mythical Distillerie Rhum A1710 in Martinique. This distillery represents a perfect balance between tradition and modernity, showcasing unparalleled craftsmanship. As one of the youngest distilleries on the island—just six years old—Rhum A1710 stands proudly among its peers, rivaling even the oldest distilleries. This small distillery is situated in a picturesque setting that reflects the passion and dreams of its creators, supported by renowned oenologists. The well-maintained grounds feature lush gardens and a welcoming atmosphere, making it an ideal place to explore the art of rum-making while enjoying various rum tastings.

At the heart of Rhum A1710 are several white rums, considered among the finest in their category. Each variety exudes remarkable finesse and enticing aromas, designed specifically for true connoisseurs. These rums are best enjoyed neat, allowing you to appreciate the complex flavors of these exceptional spirits. A visit to the distillery promises a sensual tasting experience that deepens your appreciation for the subtlety and refinement of their craft. Rhum A1710 offers a generous and memorable tasting session. From the very first sip, it's evident that this is not mass-produced rum. You can feel the quality, whether you're enjoying it in a ti-punch, as a cocktail, or neat; it sits beautifully on the palate.

Visiting Martinique is a must, especially the Distillerie Rhum A1710. The experience is enriching, intimate, and designed for those with a taste for class. Even if you're not a rum enthusiast, the tour sheds light on the entire process, from sugar cane fields to aging. While the tours are conducted in French, the friendly staff welcomes English speakers and is eager to share their knowledge and passion.

Tip

A visit to Rhum A1710 pairs wonderfully with a trip to the nearby Habitation Clément, which is also one of the most prestigious rum estates. Both locations are unique and classy, taking you on a historical journey through the rich heritage and innovative practices surrounding Martinique's rums.

Accommodations - where to stay

At Le Francois, you'll find the perfect place to stay. Here are some of the best accommodations providing good value for money, this list offers everything from luxury villas to charming bed and breakfasts.

1. **Hôtel Frégate Bleue**

 Fregate Est 4, Le Francois 97240 Martinique

Nestled in the town of François on the eastern side of Martinique, this charming boutique hotel is a mere five-minute drive from the city center. It boasts breathtaking views of the Atlantic Ocean and is situated just 50 meters from the shoreline. Visitors can relax by the outdoor pool, which is enveloped by vibrant greenery and soothing trade winds. Featuring a mix of traditional Creole design and a welcoming ambiance, it serves as a perfect getaway for a tranquil vacation.

2. **Hotel Plein Soleil**

 Pointe Thalemont Mansarde Rance, Le Francois 97240 Martinique

The main house has 16 rooms and suites with contemporary décor and plush linen, and there are five villas distributed across the 8,000 m2 garden. Every lodging has a unique personality. For example, the guest rooms have a view of the bay, while the master pool,

garden suites, and duplex suites have private pools for more seclusion and leisure.

3. **Les Hauts Du Cap**

73 Rue des Fleurs Pointe Jacob - Cap Est, Le Francois 97240 Martinique

A guest house with beautiful views of the ocean.

4. **La Maison de l'Ilet Oscar**

Ilet Oscar, Le Francois 97240 Martinique

The home of Ilet Oscar is located in the shadow of the palm trees that protect the shore, just off Francois's village, in the gentle Caribbean. The four bedrooms of the Creole home open out to "The White Lagoons" with its private pontoon, surrounded by beauty and rich in history.

5. **Les Colonnades**

Usine du Simon, Le Francois 97240 Martinique

Les Colonnades, tucked away between François and Vauclin, is a Caribbean gem that is both close to the island's stunning southern beaches and away from the throngs of tourists. There are nine distinct apartments/bungalows on this property, each with its own bathroom, pool, exercise equipment, and relaxation spaces. So get ready to be treated to a charming bed and breakfast.

6. **Villa Clemence**

 Pointe Thalemont, Le Francois 97240 Martinique

A charming and budget-friendly villa that provides a wonderful experience for its guests.

7. **L'habitation de l'Ilet Thierry**

 Bp 26, Le Francois 97240 Martinique

A stunning hotel that offers both budget-friendly and luxurious accommodations, featuring a rejuvenating spa, a state-of-the-art fitness center, and breathtaking views of the turquoise ocean.

8. **Villas Cap Est**

 Chemin Cap Est., Le Francois 97240 Martinique

This villa offers an idyllic retreat for those seeking tranquility. With its sun-drenched terrace overlooking a sparkling azure pool, guests can unwind while sipping on refreshing beverages. The soothing sounds of nature create a harmonious backdrop, inviting you to relax in cozy nooks adorned with plush cushions. A villa perfect for a serene stay.

You can also check for other accommodations here

Le Diamant

Le Diamant is a charming city in Martinique that owes its name to the iconic "Rocher du Diamant," a steep, 175-meter-high rock located over 4 kilometers off the coast, conquered, fortified, and inhabited by the English at the beginning of the 19th century for 17 months before being reconquered by the French. Nowadays, Rocher du Diamant is protected as a natural reserve, mainly for bird reproduction, and has also acquired the reputation of housing a lot of snakes.

Getting There

Le Diamant is easily reachable by car, passing along the way through very nice landscapes, which already make it worth the ride as much as the destination. From the capital Fort-de-France, just take the route nationale N5 in the direction of Rivière-Salée, then follow indications for Le Diamant. The road is 30 kilometers and usually takes 45 minutes.

If you don't have a car but depend on public means, you can use buses that are less frequent. The local bus network, in general, named "TCSP" for Transport en Commun de Martinique links several towns, of which Le Diamant is one. It is fairly cheap, but you will need to check the schedule in advance.

Getting Around

Once in Le Diamant, getting around is very easy. It is a relatively small town, with many of the major attractions within easy walking distance. To see the wider environs, a car rental is recommended; this gives one the freedom to make short drives along to sights like the beautiful beaches at Anses d'Arlet.

This narrow route between Le Diamant and Anses d'Arlet has superb views of Rocher du Diamant. For the outdoorsy visitor, cycling here equals the view in spectacle. It is ups and downs with some heavy climbing here, but this well-repaid view is especially worth the effort.

Tourist Attractions

Exploring the Waters

Due to its volcanic origin, Le Diamant represents the dream of a diver due to the richness of underwater fauna and flora, including caves. The diving clubs around the city welcome beginners, advanced divers, and everyone in between. Whether you are into exploring vibrant coral reefs, spotting exotic marine life, or taking part in underwater caving, the options to dive into adventure are abundant.

Diamond Rock

Historical landmark

 [Martinique](#)

Diamond Rock is a breathtaking basalt island standing off from the coast of Martinique by about three kilometers. It is not only a natural wonder but also a historical landmark. This dramatic rock in profile rises 175 meters high with a diameter of 300 meters and has an interesting story behind it. Most famously, during the Napoleonic Wars, it was fortified by the British and called "HMS Diamond Rock." In this case, the British equipped it with cannons and took over the waters, with French ships trying to reach Fort-de-France being decimated.

Although there were several attempts, no French troops could reclaim the rock from them, and as a matter of fact, the rock has become symbolic of British ingenuity and military strategy.

Photo by Kathleen Jarchow (unsplash)

Today, Diamond Rock has transformed from a wartime fortress to a haven for scuba divers. Its transparent waters and replete marine life make it an increasingly popular spot for underwater delves. The more adventurous can attempt dives into its surrounding depths, the rock's vibrant underwater ecosystem up close.

For those who would prefer to stay dry, the view from Vista Point itself is simply out of this world. Due to its peculiarly carved shape and the glitter it assumes at certain times of the day, the rock gives every appearance of an iceberg that is floating. It's a wondrous sight to see, especially with the backdrop of the vast Caribbean Sea.

But Diamond Rock is something more than just a view: beautiful landscapes around it-Pointe du Diamant, for instance-are ideal to take pictures from. Its rugged beauty and strategic location make this volcanic remains a rather interesting stop for the guests of Martinique.

Insider Tips

- **Stunning View**: Even if you're not into history, Diamond Rock is seriously impressive to look at. That vista point view is worth the trip alone.
- **Get Different Perspectives**: See it from the beach, a boat tour, wherever! Each angle gives you a different perspective on this unique rock.
- **Try the Le Diamanté Beach** 🏝️: If crowded beaches aren't your thing, this spot's less packed, has calm water for swimming, and you guessed it, great views of the rock.
- **Stay Safe**: Some of the beaches have strong currents. Be smart, and don't take any chances while swimming.

Photo by Claudia Mejia de la Cuz (unsplash)

Morne Larcher

Hike spot

[Le Diamant 97223, Martinique](#)

If you're visiting Martinique and love a good hike, Morne Larcher should be on your list. This iconic volcanic hill near Le Diamant offers not just a challenging ascent but also breathtaking views that make the effort worthwhile. One of its good qualities is that, while it's a known spot, it seems less crowded than some of the island's other beaches and hikes.

The Hike

Starting early in the morning is a good idea to avoid the heat and to enjoy a more peaceful climb. The path is shaded, so you won't need a hat or sunglasses. Make sure to wear sturdy hiking shoes and bring good mosquito repellent. The trail is rocky, and the ascent can feel more like climbing at times, so be prepared for a bit of adventure.

For those not used to ascent hikes, Morne Larcher can be quite challenging. Some have found it difficult and not accessible to all. However, the determination pays off when you reach the top. The panoramic view of Diamond Beach is simply magnificent. There's even a second viewpoint accessible by a small trail that descends slightly, offering even more stunning scenery.

The top of Morne Larcher offers a spectacular reward for your efforts. The view of Diamond Beach is breathtaking, and the feeling of accomplishment is unbeatable. It's a perfect spot to take a break, enjoy the scenery, and capture some amazing photos. The descent is almost as challenging as the ascent, especially if it has rained recently. Take your time to avoid slipping on wet leaves or rocks. The entire hike, including the climb and descent, typically takes about 1 hour and 50 minutes.

It is a good idea to go early in the morning, as it will not be hot yet, and you will feel more comfortable while climbing up. The path is well-shaded, so you will not need a hat or sunglasses but still take them if you feel like. Wear stout hiking shoes and bring good mosquito repellent. The trail has rocky parts, and at times, the ascent may feel more like climbing, so be ready for some adventure.

Not for the fainthearted, Morne Larcher does have its challenges, especially to those who are not used to ascent hikes. Some people finds it difficult and so it's not accessible to everyone especially if you aren't a little bit athletic. However, determination pays off once you have reached the top. Panoramic view of Diamond Beach is simply magnificent. One can even access another viewpoint by taking a small trail that goes down a bit, and the sceneries are just great.

The reward at the top of Morne Larcher is truly spectacular. Looking over Diamond Beach, it's a phenomenal sight that few will get to enjoy; secondly, the thrill of achievement must have been unparalleled. This will be a good point to rest, take in the view, and get some great shots.

The descent is almost as difficult as going up, especially if there has been recent rain. Take your time lest you slip on wet leaves or rocks. The whole hike consisting of the climb and descent would take about 1 hour and 50 minutes.

Tips for a Safe Hike

1. **Avoid Rainy Days:** The rocks can become slippery, making the hike treacherous.

2. **Go at Your Own Pace:** Whether you're an athlete or a novice, take your time. Don't get discouraged by the climb; the reward at the top is worth it.

3. **Stay Hydrated:** Bring a small bottle of water, but keep your load light.

4. **Don't Look Up Too Much:** Focus on your steps to avoid feeling overwhelmed by the climb.

5. **Use the Natural Support:** There are plenty of rocks and trees to help you along the way.

Memorial de l'Anse Caffard

Historical site

 [FX73+MCP, Le Diamant, Martinique](#)

Situated on the coast of Le Diamant in Martinique, Memorial de l'Anse Caffard is a touching tribute to the nameless slaves who lost their lives in the tragic shipwreck of 1830. Conceived by a self-taught Martinican sculptor Jean Valère, this powerful monument was erected in 1998 to commemorate the 150th anniversary of the abolition of slavery.

The striking white statues of the memorial, symbolizing mourning in the Caribbean, stand in a triangular formation. This is to symbolize the triangular trade route between Europe, Africa, and the Americas. They face 110° East, toward the Gulf of Guinea whence the ill-fated ship most likely originated. It was in the night between the 8th and 9th of April, 1830 when the slave ship, on its illegal voyage, ran onto rocks off Diamond City, killing around 300 African captives. Only six of them survived to tell these horrific tales that would be engraved in Martinican memory forever.

Many visitors find the experience emotive. The whole memorial is rather poignantly situated, overlooking the sea. Information boards in French and English outline the tragic events, therefore informing one properly of the history and significance of the site and it's for this reason that tourists are often overcome with a deep feeling of sorrow and thought during the accounts of atrocities and lives lost.

At this site, it is not only about learning history at the Memorial de l'Anse Caffard but also about feeling it. The powerful art and the historical context create a spiritual experience. The memorial stands to remind martinicans and its visitors of those who suffered during the transatlantic slave trade, of their strength and resilience. The nearby Diamond Rock Vista Point offers a contrasting serene and uplifting experience, balancing the heavy emotions with its stunning natural beauty.

Practical Tips for Visiting

- **Parking:** There is ample parking on the shoulder of the road, making it accessible for visitors.

- **Information Boards:** Detailed descriptions are provided in both French and English, enhancing the educational value of your visit.

- **Nearby Attractions:** A short drive up the road will take you to Diamond Rock Vista Point, where you can enjoy breathtaking views and reflect on the memorial's lessons in a tranquil setting.

Plage de Dizac

Beach

 [FXG7+9F5, Le Diamant 97223, Martinique](#)

Welcome to Plage de Dizac, one of the most beloved beaches in Le Diamant, Martinique. This lovely beach is a real treasure; beautiful palms and light, inviting sand make it the perfect destination. You can walk along all its length when strolling and enjoy the fabulous view of the Diamond Rock standing proudly offshore, which very often will steal your attention. Many visitors rave about walking the entire length of Plage de Dizac, enjoying the lively atmosphere of people swimming and playing in the waves. The palm trees around this beach are a big plus, allowing picnicking on the grass with shade and relaxation. And if you are lucky, far down the beach, you will find some quiet spot that will bring you even closer to the hypnotic Diamond Rock—a truly unforgettable experience.

For those planning to visit, it's wise to arrive early to secure a favorable spot, as this beach can get quite crowded, especially during peak times. The vendors near the beach offer a variety of local treats and essentials, adding to the convenience and charm of the place. However, it's important to mention that seaweeds can sometimes be bothersome, impacting the enjoyment of swimming and the beach atmosphere. Nevertheless, the stunning scenery and captivating waves make this location a top choice for surf lovers and those who enjoy strolling barefoot along the beach. A leisurely walk along the shoreline usually takes around an hour, providing a peaceful and picturesque retreat.

Photo by claire ANSART (pixabay)

Other Noteworthy Areas to Visit in Martinique

Tourist Attractions

Cap Macré

Beach

 Le Marin 97290, Martinique

If you're looking for a genuine beach experience in Martinique that avoids the tourist crowds, Cap Macré is an excellent choice. This stunning and relatively untouched beach is a little off the main paths, providing a serene retreat with breathtaking natural views.

Situated on the Atlantic coast of the island, Cap Macré is celebrated for its unrefined beauty and tranquil vibe. The beach is bordered by trees that offer abundant shade, making it a great spot for a picnic. The sand is thick, and the beach extends widely with plenty of room to either relax in the shade or soak up the sun. Because of its somewhat difficult access, Cap Macré stays mostly uncrowded, primarily attracting locals, hikers, and campers. The beach provides a feeling of privacy and calmness, making it an ideal location for a quiet day by the ocean. The natural vibe and spirit of Cap Macré foster a one-of-a-kind environment. The beach feels inviting, and the water is refreshing, offering a revitalizing break from the busy pace of life.

The untamed, lush surroundings framed by white sand and turquoise waters create a peaceful sanctuary, perfect for spending the day with family or enjoying time alone. Many tourists often comment on the enchanting hues of the sea, which can vary from emerald green to deep blue, especially in February. The beach itself features soft sand and a gentle slope, allowing for a pleasant swimming experience for individuals of all ages.

Practical Tips

- **Accessibility:** The road to Cap Macré is long, dirt, and stony, which can be a deterrent for some tourists. However, the journey is well worth it once you arrive.

- **Amenities:** There are no bars, showers, or toilets, so come prepared. Bringing your own food and drinks is essential.

- **Safety:** The sea can be rough even in good weather, so be cautious, especially with children. It's best not to venture too far from the shore on your first visit.

Le Jardin De La Montagne

Botanical garden

 Quartier coq Vauclin, 97280, Martinique

Le Jardin De La Montagne is indeed a hidden treasure in Martinique, located at the top of a small and steep route. Well off the usual tourist trails, this magnificent garden is intimate and peaceful enough for both the nature lovers and the botanic enthusiasts.

Reaching this spot is quite an adventure, but the reward at the end is every bit worth the effort. The parking is pretty accessible, though limited to about four to five spaces, emphasizing the garden's confidential and exclusive nature. So, I suggest you take the "high" roads when you decide on navigating such challenging terrains. Le Jardin De La Montagne is a tapestry of vibrant flowers and unique plant species. The Valley of Porcelain Roses is the highlight-one can hardly believe the beauty of it all. So many plants and flowers are packed along the shaded pathways, each one so unusual, that some of them even seem to be out of this world. Its dominant viewpoints offer stunning views, thus rendering every moment spent in this garden picture-perfect.

What sets this garden apart is the guided tour offered by the devoted owner. Most tourists who visit this flower oasis continually laud the friendly welcome and intriguing explanations provided by the owner. With an interesting and versatile approach, he calls your attention to the vast range of plants within the garden. From the time you arrive, you're treated to a delightful refreshment, setting the tone for an amazing experience. The approximately one-hour tour immerses you in the brilliant richness of the island's vegetation. Unlike the more commercial Balata Gardens, Le Jardin de La Montagne offers a more personal and private experience, making it a must-visit for those seeking a genuine connection with nature.

Petit Anse

Beach

In Martinique, Petit Anse is a village that is really attractive and assures a real and pleasant experience. It is well hospitable, and filled with generous people that make you feel at home the moment you enter. The beach is one of the main attractions here in Petit Anse, literally set right in the middle of the village. The beach is sometimes crowded, like all other beaches during high season, but it is a very nice spot to rest and enjoy the water. At the end of the pontoon, there is a great view over the church in the village-which is worth seeing.

One of the highlights in Petit Anse is access to a fishing port where one can buy very fresh fish directly from the fishermen. Along the beach in the village, one finds quite a number of restaurants that offer several mouth-watering dishes out of which many feature fishes labelled as the catch of the day.

To the right of the shore, the outcropping rocks are literally teeming with life in the water-even starfish-for the adventurous. It is highly recommended for snorkeling, so bring a float or some water wings for maximum enjoyment. The water is clear and inviting at this spot, just right for a refreshing swim. In addition, the village is home to a number of species of birds, including hummingbirds and pelicans, that contribute to further tranquility and naturalness. Watching a pelican plunge among the swimmers is a sight to behold.

Practical Tips

Visit in the Afternoon: Schedule your visit for around 4 PM if you wish to get the famous picture of the church with the sun behind you.

Shade and Sun Protection: There isn't much shade on the beach, so either carry an umbrella or pick a position beneath the large tree on the right side of the beach.

Underwater Life: The village has put in place a rock that promotes underwater life, together with explanatory buoys that provide information about the local plants and animals.

Rhum Saint James

Rum distillery

 7 VC de Bezaudin, Sainte-Marie 97230, Martinique

Opening hours: 9:00am – 5:00pm

Welcome to Rhum Saint James, which is ideally set in the heart of Sainte Marie in Martinique. This enchanting estate offers an immersive journey through the history and craftsmanship of Saint James rum; for this reason, no true connoisseur or curious traveler should miss this site. Your trip begins at the

Musée du Rhum, which houses an intriguing assembly of stills and other historical artifacts. The museum provides in-depth explanations of the distillation process and the rich history of Saint-James rum. Although exhibits are in French, this is certainly a wonderful visual adventure.

To maximize your experience, allow at least two hours to view in full what Rhum Saint James has to offer as you plan your visit here. Take your casual walk around the manicured gardens, then take in the architectural design of the distillery complex and sample some fine rum—this is one plantation house that will make for a very enjoyable and enriching experience. One highlight of the visit is the meandering little train ride that takes you through cane plantations bathed in sunlight and framing postcard-perfect images of the countryside. You'll finally come to the beautifully restored Habitation La Salle, where you'll be able to visit the Atelier du Rhum and the chais (barrel rooms). For those wishing to delve a little deeper, take a guided tour during the sugar campaign when the distillery is in full swing. The well-informed staffs will take you through all aspects of the rum-making process, from cane to bottle. This tour often ends with a tasting session at the end where a variety of different types of rums are available to taste. You could also purchase some vintage rums before you leave, although the pricing of certain rum bottles has raised questions about value as they can be gotten at a lower price outside the museum.

The bar itself has a cozy atmosphere and an extended tasting menu for purists and first-timers alike. Afterwards, take the time to unwind in the estate's tranquil park or visit the small craft shop in search of unique gifts. The estate also has a very nice restaurant that is highly recommended for its flavorful regional dishes; an excellent place to spend a leisurely lunch.

Galleria Commercial Center: A Modern Shopping Experience in Le Lamentin

[Acajou S, Le Lamentin 97232, Martinique](#)

The Galleria Commercial Centre in Le Lamentin is ultramodern by Caribbean standards, having a feel for shopping. Be it high-end products or commodities of everyday use, Galleria has it all. It stands out amongst all the malls due to its attached grocery store. The range and quality are amazing, enabling one to get all they want under one roof. One can never find a problem with parking here because the mall has a huge number of parking spots for its visitors. From fast food items to fine dining, one can find ample numbers of eatery places in this mall to fulfill any type of craving. Along with food, the mall also comprises a big grocery shop and an endless number of stores selling anything that you can ever imagine. Wonderful flooring adds a bit of class to your shopping. Public transportation is available from Fort-de-France, and the stop for the MOZAIK airport bus line is right at the mall. Taxis are also easily available; therefore, there is no problem reaching or returning from the mall.

The Galleria Commercial Center is new, spacious, clean, and has two floors. The number of shops it hosts is rather large, among them being Galeries Lafayette and the well-known Hyper U. The mall has some fun places to dine and is connected directly to a hotel, giving visitors an easy transition. As expected from a modern mall, Galleria offers all the usual services: an information kiosk, restrooms, rental services, and more. These facilities ensure a comfortable and convenient visit for all shoppers.

Grand Anse d'Arlet

Beach

 [Les Anses-d'Arlet, Martinique](#)

Grand Anse d'Arlet is a stunning destination in Martinique, ideal for a memorable beach day. This beach is a snorkeler's paradise, especially suitable for beginners. Just about 50 feet from the shore, you'll find a rocky area filled with colorful fish. For added convenience, consider taking the ferry from the cruise port; however, be aware that the beach closes on Saturdays, which means there are no loungers or chairs available on that day. If you're driving, parking is easy with a grassy car park located at the end of the street near the three islets.

The beach itself has a gentle slope into the water, making it safe but deep enough for a refreshing swim. Although Grand Anse d'Arlet isn't always crowded, a perfect time to visit is in May which is the low season and a treat with very few people around. So, unlike the crowded small coves, Grand Anse d'Arlet provides a serene and pretty sheltered beach experience.

While at this haven, don't miss the obligatory photo opportunity with the small church facing the pontoon—it's a symbol of Martinique. The newly opened Kalua restaurant near the pier is also highly recommended for delicious local cuisine. Snorkeling here is a highlight, with sea turtles casually grazing on the seagrasses just meters from the shore. Whether you visit during the week for a peaceful escape or the weekend when it's livelier, Grand Anse d'Arlet never disappoints. This beach truly encapsulates the essence of Martinique's natural beauty and tranquil charm, making it a must-visit destination for any traveler.

Anse Noire

Beach

 [GWG7+X2, Les Anses-d'Arlet 97217, Martinique](GWG7+X2,%20Les%20Anses-d'Arlet%2097217,%20Martinique)

Best time to visit: 8:00 am

This is another beautiful beach located in the southern part of Martinique. Nestled next to its more famous neighbor, Anse Dufour, Anse Noire offers a captivating and tranquil escape for those seeking a unique beach experience in Martinique. Known for its picturesque black sand and serene ambiance, this small cove is a hidden gem worth exploring.

Scenic Beauty and Snorkeling Adventures

Anse Noire is a beautiful black sand beach, set against dramatic cliffs that plunge into the azure sea. The wooden pontoon provides a perfect spot to dive into the water. Early in the morning, snorkeling here is a delight, with opportunities to see fish to the right of the pontoon and, if you're lucky, turtles to the left. The clear, sunny weather enhances the snorkeling experience, allowing you to witness the vibrant marine life up close.

Accessibility and Amenities

Accessing Anse Noire involves a bit of effort, as you'll need to descend (and later ascend) about 137 steps to return to the parking lot. This might sound daunting, but the reward is well worth it. Unlike Anse Dufour, Anse Noire is less crowded, offering a more peaceful atmosphere. It's advisable to arrive early to secure a parking spot along the road or at the small parking lot at the top. Remember to park in the direction of your departure to make the exit smoother.

While Anse Noire lacks the dining and drinking options found at Anse Dufour, it makes up for it with its natural charm. You can rent kayaks and paddleboards on the beach, adding to the adventure. However, it's wise to bring your own refreshments and snacks to fully enjoy your day.

Practical Tips and Local Advice

For the best experience, consider visiting Anse Noire early in the morning or around noon when vacationers are less likely to crowd the beach. This timing not only helps you avoid the rush but also provides a better chance to find parking and enjoy the beach in its natural state.

While some visitors have expressed disappointment due to the small size and crowded conditions during peak times, others find Anse Noire to be one of Martinique's most beautiful coves. Its charm lies in its wild, untouched feel, and the refreshing shade provided by coconut and palm trees.

Insider Tips

- Parking is notoriously tricky, so be prepared for a challenge. This beach is definitely worth it if snorkeling's your thing, but lazy sunbathers might want to try other spots.
- Pack water, snacks, and any gear you want. There are rentals nearby, but no proper facilities on the beach itself.
- Don't be put off by the black sand at first – it's volcanic and totally cool! This beach is small, but the payoff is the amazing snorkeling and fewer crowds.
- That black sand gets HOT! Shoes or flip-flops are a must to avoid burning your soles.
- There are steep stairs and rocks to get to the beach, so be aware if you have mobility issues.

Anse Figuier

Beach

 [Le Marin 97211, Martinique](#)

Welcome to Anse Figuier, one of the most picturesque beaches of Martinique carrying all the hallmarks of peace. In this guide, you will explore everything that you should know for an unforgettable visit to this charming destination.

Getting there

Access to Anse Figuier is easy. Your vehicle can be parked in the nearby asphalt parking lot free of charge. Arrive early, especially at weekends, and you are assured of having a place in the shade because the beach fills up fast with locals. This is a dreamy beach with tranquil waters and soft sands. It has a peaceful atmosphere, best to avoid the crowd of people (only on weekdays). This would be a very good place for families since its gentle waters are perfect for the little children and also a hidden corner where mostly natives are found. If you love snorkeling, then bring your equipment to see the various bursting marine life.

Cleanliness on this beach is among the first things you will notice, in the morning, a rake is passed, and there are plenty of trash cans to help keep the area as spotless as possible. The coconut trees are even pruned so the nuts don't fall for safety reasons to make sure this environment is as pleasant as it is safe.

Marine activities

The snorkeling side of the beach runs along the rocky coast on the west side and is really amazing because of the huge variety of fish. Kids and adults alike will be really excited by such an adventure. However, be prepared that sometimes the water can be cloudy, and you may catch more plastic than fish-which can be a disappointment.

Places to Eat

Dining-wise, there are a few scattered options around Anse Figuier to suit all budgets. A must-try place is **Le Cabanon**, a small and friendly restaurant that welcomes everybody. One can certainly enjoy a superb meal at this restaurant on the shaded terrace with a great view overlooking the beach: the Ti punch, accras, smoked chicken, and grilled fish are all great, not to mention the ice cream.

Le Musee de la Banane (Banana Museum)

Museum

[Quartier, Fourniols, Sainte-Marie 97230, Martinique](#)

Opening hours: 9:00 AM - 5:00 PM

Entry fee: around 14 euros

Welcome to Le Musée de la Banane, a quaint museum set in a working plantation that takes one through all things about bananas-from the minute details of the harvest all through to the packing process, even on to the artistic expression of bananas on pottery and art. This is a nice stop for anyone taking in the sights around Martinique's lush landscape.

The museum offers a great combination of educational input and natural attractiveness. While strolling around the park, one will notice several species of bananas, over 300 varieties emanating from Asia, Africa, the Pacific, and even Martinique, among other interesting plants. The museum also has a very nice park, therefore making an excursion pleasant to be enjoyed outdoors.

The museum offers an educational and tasting experience, providing insightful information about bananas, though much of this is concentrated at the entrance. While you are there you have the chance to taste some bananas, but on some days, the variety might be limited to the common Cavendish, but try not to miss the opportunity to taste unique banana-based products like banana ketchup. The. With an entry fee of about 14 Euros, this captivating scenery provides unique insights that makes your visit worthwhile. Since it's mostly outdoors, the museum is best visited on a good weather day and is stroller-friendly, making it ideal for families with young children. The plantation also sells various food products and souvenirs, though some are not locally produced.

An Mao Jardin paysager & historique

Historical site

[Morne Gommier Marin, 97290, Martinique](#)

Visits: By appointment only

Appointment Website: [An Mao](#)

A Journey Through History and Nature

An Mao Jardin Paysager & Historique, officially known as An Mao: The Inheritance of the Ancestors, is located in the heart of Martinique. This park is rich in history and culture, as it was once inhabited by runaway slaves and later by those who were newly emancipated. Through its gardens and attractions, An Mao celebrates and preserves ancestral knowledge, emphasizing the vital roles of trees, plants, legends, and faith in the sociocultural development of Martinique.

Pierre-Yves, your guide and narrator. Upon arrival, you will be welcomed by Pierre-Yves, whose personal story is intertwined with the rich history of Martinique. He then escorts you along the "**chemin des ancêtres**" and gives an emotional ode to his ancestors, Africans who were brought to the island as slaves. His is not a mere informative story, but a vastly touching one with bringing history alive through his deep knowledge of medicinal plants and their use and unforgettable stories of growing up on this land. This is not only a tour of the exterior-through the nature of Martinique-but it is also an interior one, through the heart of Martinique's cultural heritage.

Most tourist that come here all leave with the story of Pierre-Yves and a message of humanity tucked in their hearts. The tour becomes emotionally enriching due to his passion and humility. Many have described the visit as a journey of change, being much closer to the history of Martinique and more at peace by the end of the visit.

Practical Tips

Appointment Only Remember, An Mao works on an appointment-only basis, ensuring a personalized and intimate experience.

Plan Your Visit Consider starting your stay in Martinique with a visit to An Mao. It's an ideal way to immerse yourself in the island's history and culture right from the beginning.

Be Prepared for a Journey The drive to An Mao is part of the adventure. Trust the signs and be ready for a short walk to reach this hidden gem.

Palais de Justice

Historical site

[35 Bd Général de Gaulle, Fort-de-France 97200, Martinique](#)

If you find yourself in Fort-de-France, the Palais de Justice is a notable landmark worth a visit. This neoclassical courthouse, built in 1906, stands proudly in the heart of the old town, offering a glimpse into the island's legal history and architectural charm. While the building itself might not be an architectural masterpiece, it exudes a certain solidity and quaint appeal. The front garden, well-enclosed, features a statue of Victor Schoelcher, a key political figure and benefactor of Martinique, making it a worthwhile spot for a quick stop and photo.

As you explore the interior passageways, you'll come across various artifacts and two significant declarations accompanied by photos of Camille Darsières, another important Martinican politician. These elements add a layer of historical depth to your visit. From the courthouse, a pretty pathway leads you towards Cour Perrinon, enhancing the overall experience.

Do note, however, that the garden area has been a site for protests against chlordécone, a controversial pesticide issue on the island. Despite this, the Palais de Justice remains a point of reference in Fort-de-France, offering a short but meaningful visit that captures a slice of Martinique's heritage.

Presqu'ile de la Caravelle

Hike Spot

[Q34Q+FVR, La Trinité, Martinique](#)

Presqu'ile de la Caravelle in Martinique offers an unforgettable hiking experience with a variety of stunning views and landscapes, including rocky shorelines, cliffs, and serene mangroves. This hike is a top highlight of any trip to Martinique, and it can be for you too! There are three trail options to choose from: the full 8km loop for a complete adventure, the middle distance 6km route that cuts off the headland for a balanced terrain experience, and the short 2km trail focused only on the mangroves for a quick nature fix. You can take the 6km hike, which could last about 2 hours and 45 minutes due to the rough terrain, photo stops, and having a good chat along the way. The paths are well-marked with blue and white painted discs, making navigation easy.

Given the high cliffs, this hike is best for older kids and adults. It's advisable to avoid wet weather as the volcanic rocks can become slippery. Walk clockwise to end at the chateau for refreshments, which closes at 4:30 PM and requires a small fee. For parking, drive further past the bitumen to a second car park before the gate for easier access. Proper footwear is essential; training shoes are adequate, but hiking boots can be more comfortable. Bring water, sunscreen, and a hat, as the heat can be overwhelming, especially later in the day. Rain can make some sections muddy and slippery, particularly near the cliffs.

The Experience

We started our hike from the farthest parking lot, opting to begin at the lighthouse path, tackling the toughest parts first and finishing with a refreshing swim at the beach. We left at 9:30 AM, which was too late; an early start is highly recommended to avoid the midday heat. The hike offers alternating passages through lush forests, mangroves, and dry landscapes. The elevation gain is around 250 meters but feels more due to the continuous ups and downs. Despite the challenges, the breathtaking views and diverse nature are well worth the effort.

Tips

So, start your hike early to avoid the heat and secure parking. If you choose the small loop, consider extending your hike to Treasure Bay Beach for a cool-off. Beware of yen-yen flies that can be a nuisance.

Embarking on the Presqu'ile de la Caravelle hike to explore the stunning natural beauty of Martinique is one of a kind experience. Whether you're a seasoned hiker or a casual walker, this hike offers a memorable adventure with its diverse landscapes and scenic views.

Anse Dufour

Beach

[*Les Anses-d'Arlet 97217, Martinique*](#)

A Haven of Tropical Peace Martinique's Anse Dufour is a unique type of beach that offers serene, pristine waters ideal for swimming and snorkeling, especially for beginners. This charming location is well known for its abundant marine life, particularly the sea turtles who call it home. Golden-white sands and a peaceful atmosphere await you when you arrive. Due to its tiny size, the beach can get crowded, particularly in the afternoon. To guarantee a nice parking space along the road and take in the peace before the throngs arrive, plan to arrive early, **preferably between 7 and 8 am.** A quick 5-minute stroll down a flight of stairs leads to the beach.

Marine Life and Snorkeling

At Anse Dufour, snorkeling is a must-do activity. Beautiful corals, vibrant fish, and of course, the well-known sea turtles abound in these waters. Early in the morning, when the seas are clear and the turtles are more active, is the ideal time of day to snorkel. To prevent upsetting the turtles, remember to maintain a polite 5-meter minimum distance from them.

Insider tips

A few facilities are available in Anse Dufour to enhance your stay. After swimming, you may have a refreshing drink or a bite to eat at the on-site restaurant and bar. There isn't much cover, though, so wear an anti-UV t-shirt or lots of sunscreen to protect yourself from the sun.

- ➤ **Arrive Early:** To beat the crowds and find parking easily, arrive between 7am and 8am.
- ➤ **Parking:** Park in the direction of your return to make departure smoother.
- ➤ **Snorkeling Gear:** Bring your own snorkel gear to fully enjoy the underwater sights.
- ➤ **Turtle Etiquette:** Maintain a 5-meter distance from the turtles to ensure their safety and your own.
- ➤ **Sunscreen:** Use reef-safe sunscreen or wear an anti-UV t-shirt to protect the marine environment.
- ➤ **Alternative Spot:** For a less crowded experience, visit the nearby Anse Noire, a black sand beach just a 10-minute walk away.

Distillerie J M

Rum distillery

 Fond Préville, Macouba 97218, Martinique

Opening hours: 9:00 AM - 5:00 PM

Situated in the lush, isolated valleys of northern Martinique, Distillerie J.M offers a captivating blend of history, culture, and natural beauty. Established in the 18th century, this distillery is one of the island's most treasured landmarks. Let's embark on a journey to uncover the rich history and unique experiences that await you at Distillerie J.M.

The history of Distillerie J.M started back in 1790, when Antoine Leroux-Préville purchased the estate. In 1845, Jean-Marie Martin purchased the habitation-sucrerie Fonds-Préville and gave it the brand name J.M by using his initials. Generations passed, and the family Crassous de Médeuil further enhanced the quality and fame of J.M rhum. The distillery joined GBH in 2002, while in 2013, a major renovation at the production facilities gave an immersive experience for visitors.

The Distillery Experience

A visit to the Distillerie J.M. really engages all the senses: admission is free, and one may take a self-guided tour, lasting about 30 minutes, through a small representative sugar cane plantation through the impressive machinery of the process of rhum making, from fermentation through distillation to storage. One is surrounded by the authentic sounds and aromas of rhum production, thus getting a true taste of Martinique heritage.

At the end of the tour, you will reach the tasting bar where you will get to taste four different J.M rhums. Tastings are free; of course, you can buy bottles or miniatures-great to take a piece of Martinique home. For those traveling with limited space in your luggage, the miniature boxes-including six different drinks with tasting notes-offer an economic alternative.

Practical Tips and Notes

- **Accessibility:** Some parts of the estate may be under renovation, so check ahead if you want to see specific areas.

- **Location:** The distillery is quite remote, situated in the far north of the island, making it a peaceful and scenic destination.

- **Welcome:** Visitors consistently praise the warm and excellent welcome, making your visit even more enjoyable.

- **Planning Your Visit:** The distillery is far from Fort-de-France, so plan your trip accordingly. Consider combining your visit with other nearby attractions to make the most of your journey.

- **Double Your Adventure**: Pair this trip with a visit to Mount Pelée for a seriously adventurous day out!
- **Try Other Distilleries:** For rum lovers, try adding on a visit to Depaz distillery. Different setting, different rums – double the fun!

Domaine d'Emeraude

Botanical garden

 PVXX+P9R, Le Morne Rouge 97260, Martinique

Entrance fee: about 9 euros

Situated on the northern part of Martinique, Domaine d'Emeraude is a tranquil botanical garden and a nature reserve, which in any case offers another perspective of immediately plunging one into nature. Although it is not as big as the Balata Garden, it has its own charm and is worth visiting in case one wants to plunge into the flora and fauna of the island without too many tourists around.

It has a very well-curated museum where information about the numerous plants and animals of the region is in a both fun and instructive way, but alas only in French. The main attraction of Domaine d'Emeraude is its three well-marked forest trails. Those vary from 30 minutes up to an hour and a half in length and thus are accessible for every fitness level. Concreted and well-maintained paths, but some hilly terrain and steps.

You'll walk these trails accompanied by the chirping of birds, the view of many species of trees and plants, and generally the beauty of a well-preserved forest. For many people, this experience is well priced at an excellent value. There is also a small gift shop in this garden and a restaurant to keep you refreshed after your walk.

Less crowded than Balata, the garden nonetheless offers a rich and rewarding experience. The landscaped park shows off the beauty of Martinican vegetation, while the wilder parts afford a more natural atmosphere of peace and quiet. The friendly staff adds to making your visit welcoming even on days when the weather is not at its best.

So, it doesn't matter if you're exploring the medicinal plants or simply enjoying the sights and sounds of nature, Domaine d'Emeraude offers a breath of fresh air and a deeper appreciation of Martinique's natural beauty. Allow yourself about **two hours** to fully enjoy all that this hidden gem has to offer.

Anse Couleuvre

Natural reserve & beach

Martinique

Nestled in the northern Caribbean coast of Martinique, Anse Couleuvre is a hidden gem that promises an unforgettable experience for beach lovers, hikers, and history enthusiasts alike. This secluded spot offers pristine natural beauty, rich history, and a variety of activities that cater to every type of traveler.

Getting There

The adventure starts with how to reach Anse Couleuvre. From the main town of St-Pierre, take the famous scenic N2 road onto D10. You drive through lush landscapes and the charming town of Saint-Pierre, famous for its rich history-the devastating 1902 eruption of Montagne Pelée. The closer you get to Anse Couleuvre, the narrower and steeper the road gets, adding a pinch of thrill to your drive. This place has very limited parking, so arrive early. Be prepared for parking along the road or in the tiny, dead-end car park and enjoy your walk through the forest down to the beach, which takes approximately 10 minutes.

Historical Highlights

En route to Anse Couleuvre, the remains of Habitation Sucrière Couleuvre-a plantation founded in 1651-are seen. For sure, this is a place full of history: during centuries, it has seen three types of agronomy, namely sugar and cocoa farming, then finally rum production and distillation of essential oils. It was abandoned in 1944 after the economic crisis and the eruption of Mount Pelée. Ruins like this are fascinating to explore and show glimpses of the colonial past of the island.

Beachside

Anse Couleuvre certainly wins with dramatic black volcanic sand and crystal-clear waters. The real jungle that surrounds you makes this a wild beach with an untouched feel that is just perfect for those seeking tranquility. It is wide and shady, with perfect picnicking and resting facilities. The waters are crystal clear, perfect for snorkeling, especially at the far-right side where you will clearly see turtles, diodons, gorgonians, and sea urchins. Bring your snorkel gear, lots of water, and snacks since there are no amenities on site.

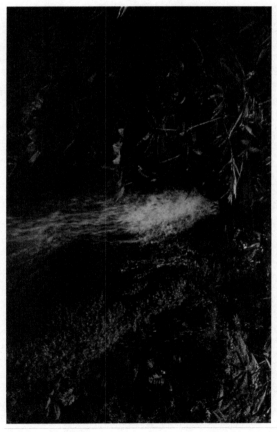

The waterfall

If you are feeling adventurous, take the 1.4 km hike from the beach up to the Couleuvre waterfall. It is an exhausting stage of walking but well worth the effort. You will be trekking through the tropical forest of the island. You might glimpse some Matoutous, which are the island's endemic tarantulas, and several fords over the Couleuvre River. Being one of the highest waterfalls in Martinique, this would be a great refreshing area where one could cool off with a swim. Do not forget to take breaks and stop for photos and picnics by the falls.

Those who want a more serious experience can make the 15-kilometer hike to Grande Rivière. This is a very demanding trail that offers tremendous views and affords the opportunity to completely throw oneself into the island's varied landscapes.

On your way back, consider taking the scenic route through the heights of Piton du Carnet. This route offers breathtaking views of the mountainous landscape and a series of winding turns that make for an exciting drive.

Tips for Your Visit

- **Footwear:** Wear sturdy walking shoes or old sneakers suitable for hiking.

- **Essentials:** Bring plenty of water, snacks, a picnic, and snorkeling gear.

- **Timing:** Arrive early to secure parking and enjoy the beach before it gets crowded.

- **Safety:** Drive carefully on the narrow and steep roads leading to Anse Couleuvre.

Les Gorges de la Falaise

Natural reserve

 [Chem. de Semaine, Ajoupa-Bouillon 97216, Martinique](#)

Opening hours: 8am – 2pm

Entrance fee: €10

Looking for another unforgettable adventure in Martinique? Les Gorges de la Falaise is the perfect escape! Nestled in the heart of the island's lush rainforest, this natural wonder offers a refreshing and exhilarating experience for visitors of all ages.

Like many activities in Martinique, it's best to arrive early to avoid the crowds. The entrance fee is 10 euros, which covers parking, access to the private domain, and a guided tour by experienced and friendly guides.

Photo by Andrew Tom (unsplash)

Before you begin this adventure make sure to bring your walking shoes or old sneakers, as they will definitely get wet. The hike starts with a descent towards the river, where you can take a moment to admire the surrounding rainforest and listen to the birds singing. Walking through the water between high rock walls is a thrilling experience. At one point, you'll need to climb a metal ladder within the watercourse, which might be a bit challenging for less athletic visitors. However, your guide will be there to ensure your safety and make you feel at ease.

The highlight of the hike is reaching the beautiful waterfall at the end of the gorge. For the adventurous, passing under the waterfall or viewing it from above is a rewarding experience. The water level can vary depending on recent weather, so be prepared for different conditions.

This outing is perfect for families, including children aged 10 and up. The path is generally manageable for everyone, and the guides are known for their friendly and reassuring demeanor.

Practical Tips

> ➤ **Bring:** Waterproof shoes
> ➤ **Cost:** 10 euros per adult
> ➤ **Duration:** About 2 hours
> ➤ **Best Time:** Early in the day

Spas
Wellness & Relaxation in Martinique

Martinique offers yoga, meditation, and other wellness retreats all over the island. Practice mindfulness with experienced instructors, surrounded by stunning natural beauty – it's the perfect way to recharge.

After a very long day or if you have been craving for a deep tissue relaxation. Martinique has great spas that deliver these services with the very best Caribbean touch. These spas on the island combine cutting-edge treatments with age-old Caribbean healing methods. Using locally obtained items like sea salt, coconut oil, and tropical fruits, these spas provide a distinctive and organic way to unwind.

1. Bod'lanmè SPA URBAN

Résidence hôtelière Poséidon Caraïbe, Rue Moi Laminaire, Fort-de-France 97200, Martinique

Opening Hours: 10:00 AM - 6:00 PM

2. La Villa Victoria

99 Rte de Ravine Vilaine, Fort-de-France 97200, Martinique

Opening Hours: 8:30 AM - 7:00 PM

3. Aux Bains De Cluny & Spa

Espace Lacaye, 1 Av. Du Grand Paradis, Schoelcher 97233, Martinique

Opening Hours: 8:30 AM - 6:00 PM

4. Eden Paradise Eco Lodges & Spa

D36 Villa Volcart, D36, Sainte-Luce 97228, Martinique

Opening Hours: 10:00 AM - 5:00 PM

5. Ang'Elle Massage

Plage n°, 6 de Dizac, Le Diamant 97223, Martinique

Opening Hours: 8:30 AM - 5:00 PM

6. Alternative Zen

Route de Mayo, Le François 97240, Martinique

Opening Hours: 8:00 AM - 6:00 PM

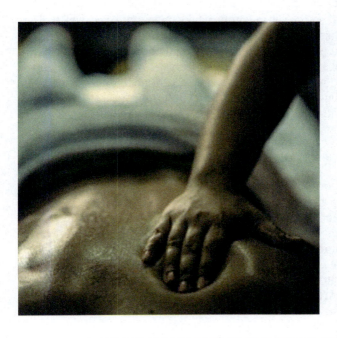

Itineraries

One Week in Martinique: A Full Week of Exploration

Day 1: Discovering Fort-de-France

Begin your Martinique journey with a fulfilling breakfast at **BBR, Beach Blue Rock,** where you can admire the beautiful beachfront views. After your meal, take a walk to the **Schoelcher Library**, an architectural wonder brimming with historical and cultural treasures. Stroll through the lively streets of Fort-de-France, and for lunch, visit **Le Cocotier** for some tasty casual Caribbean dishes. As night falls, treat yourself to an upscale dinner at **Le M**, famous for its delicious French-Caribbean seafood.

Day 2: Adventures in the North

Start your day with a delightful breakfast at **Restaurant Plein Soleil** before setting off on a hike up Mount Pelée, which offers stunning sweeping views of the island. Once you've reached the top, take time to explore the historic ruins of Saint-Pierre, highlighting the island's volcanic history. Enjoy a quick, delicious lunch at **Restaurant La Kabananou.** For dinner, indulge in a variety of flavors at **Restaurant 1643,** which provides a blend of French, Caribbean, and international cuisines.

Day 3: A Dive into History & Culture

Kick off your morning with a soothing breakfast at **Café Del Mar**, and then delve into Martinique's rich heritage at **La Savane des Esclaves**, a museum focused on the island's slave history. Keep the momentum going with a visit to the **Memorial de l'Anse Caffard**, a moving tribute to the slave trade. Recharge with a light lunch at Restaurant **SNACK BOUBOU BOKITS.** Finish your day with a delightful dinner at **Les Arômes,** offering contemporary French-Caribbean cuisine.

Day 4: Embracing Nature

Start your day with breakfast at O' Coup d'Coeur before exploring the lush **Jardin de Balata,** a stunning botanical garden filled with exotic flora and picturesque paths. After enjoying the sights, unwind on the beautiful sands of **Plage des Salines.** For lunch, opt for something quick and delicious at Pizzbook. In the evening, dine at The Yellow, where you'll find healthy dishes infused with French-Caribbean flavors.

Day 5: Art & Rum Experience

Savor breakfast at Baguet Shop - Trois-Ilets before visiting **Habitation Clement,** where you can appreciate its art collection and well-preserved estate. Take a distillery tour and sample their famous rums. For a late lunch, head to Poyo Rico for tasty local cuisine. Wrap up your day with dinner at **Le Zandoli - La Suite Villa**, merging French and Caribbean culinary traditions for a unique dining experience.

Day 6: Wildlife Exploration & Snorkeling

Begin with a cozy breakfast at La Maison Rousse before visiting the **Zoo de Martinique** to see diverse exotic wildlife in a natural environment. Then make your way to Diamond Rock for some top-notch snorkeling or diving activities. For a quick lunch, stop by Anba Fey Tol La. Treat yourself to an unforgettable dinner at **Kay Ali,** celebrated for its gourmet French dishes.

Day 7: Relaxation in the South

On your final day, start with a leisurely breakfast at your hotel. Next, unwind on the serene beach of **Anse Dufour,** known for its clear waters and vibrant marine life. Discover **Habitation Céron** to see the enormous ancient tree and explore the grounds. Enjoy a casual lunch at Ti Cozy. Conclude your trip with a splendid French dinner at **Delim's,** ensuring you end your Martinique adventure on a high note.

Practical information

When planning your trip to Martinique, there are a few key things to keep in mind to ensure a smooth and enjoyable experience.

Health Info and COVID Regulations

As Martinique is a French department, European travelers should carry their European Health Insurance Card (EHIC) to cover any necessary healthcare treatments while on the island. Keep in mind that some medical expenses may not be fully covered, and costs can vary depending on the doctor's status.

First and foremost, it's important to know that there are no mandatory vaccinations required for entry. However, if you're coming from a country at risk, it might be wise to consider vaccinations for hepatitis A and yellow fever. Thankfully, all COVID-19 related travel restrictions were lifted in August 2022, so you won't need to worry about tests or vaccinations for that either.

Safety

Speaking generally, Martinique is very safe; it is nonetheless always good practice to be cautious. Do not leave any valuables visible in your car, do not take out big sums of money from ATMs, and also take care of your belongings while at the beach. Anything can be stolen, though that rarely happens; it is better to be safe than sorry, anyway. The main risks here are related to the sun, heat, mosquito bites, and occasionally, poisonous plants or unsupervised swimming spots.

During your stay, protect yourself against the intense sun and the heat by avoiding dehydration, wearing hats, sunglasses, and sunscreen. If you're a hike enthusiast, come along with some hiking boots. As for mosquitoes, well, they are a real nuisance. To keep them away, use repellent products against mosquitoes and wear long garments; if necessary, sleep under a mosquito net.

Travel With Children

Traveling with children in Martinique is straightforward as most accommodations are child-friendly, and many restaurants offer kids' menus. Just remember to protect the little ones from mosquito bites, wild waves during your stay at the beach, and sun exposure.

Travel With Pets

If you're traveling with pets, ensure they have a pet passport issued by an authorized vet, an electronic identification chip, and up-to-date rabies vaccinations. This will make the travel process smoother for your furry friend.

Communication and Emergency Contacts

For communication, Martinique has robust internet and mobile network services. Most hotels, restaurants, and even the airport provide Wi-Fi access. Phone numbers in Martinique have ten digits and start with +596 for both landlines and mobiles.

Emergency contacts

1. **Centre Hospitalier Universitaire de Fort de France:**

: Le Meynard, Fort de France, Martinique

: +596 0596 75 15 75

: http://www.chu-martinique.fr

2. **Sea Rescue (CROSSAG):**

: Martinique

: sarcontacts.info/countries/martinique/

📞 : +596 596633333, +596 596 73 16 16

3. **Pompiers (Fire Department)**

- 📞 : '18' on a local telephone.

4. **POLICE - Gendarmerie Nationale (National Police):**

- 📞 : '17' or 05 96 59 90 00
- 📞 : +596 596 59 90 00

Money Matters

Regarding finances, Martinique uses the Euro, just like mainland France. While some establishments accept US dollars, traveler's checks, and credit cards, non-local checks might be refused. The cost of living is higher than in mainland France, so plan your budget accordingly. Prices drop during the low season but peak around Christmas and Carnival.

Language and local life

In Martinique, everything is adapted to the tropics, with the usual temperature of 28°C (82°F) throughout the year. The rainy season falls between June and November, while the dry one is from December to May. The latter is often considered the best time to visit due to its pleasant weather.

French and Creole patois are predominant, but you will find that quite a number of locals speak English, especially around the tourist areas.

By keeping these practical tips in mind, you'll be well-prepared to enjoy the vibrant culture, stunning landscapes, and warm hospitality that Martinique has to offer. Safe travels!

Martinique Month-by-Month: Festivals & Fun

January

- **New Year's Day (January 1):** The island starts the year with parties and good wishes.

- **Epiphany (La Fête des Rois):** Bakeries fill up with delicious galette des rois cakes – it's like a sweet treasure hunt to find the hidden figurine!

- **Carnival Soley Sud (January 7):** Get ready for colors, music, and pure joy as Carnival season begins!

- **Festy'Roi (January 7):** Get the Carnival party started in Le Lamentin! Expect tons of costumes, parades, and a lively atmosphere.

- **Foyal Parade (January 14):** The capital city kicks off its Carnival celebrations in style. Grab your best costume and join the fun!

- **Night Parade in Dillon (January 20):** Experience the magic of Carnival after dark – think costumes, lights, and a totally different energy!

February/March

- **Candlemas Day (February 2):** While not a huge celebration in Martinique, it's a recognized religious festival honoring the presentation of Christ in the Temple.

- **Bèt à fé (February 3):** Get ready for lights, costumes, and Carnival music! This nighttime parade in Fort-de-France is another great way to get into the festive spirit.

- **Schoelcher Nautical Week (February 13):** Sailors from all over the Caribbean (and France) compete in thrilling races on those gorgeous blue waters.

- **Carnival (February 14):** Five crazy days of parades, costumes, and non-stop celebrations! Mardi Gras is the wild finale.

- **Ash Wednesday:** While other carnivals wind down, Martinique's keeps going! They say goodbye to "King Carnival" with somber parades and a fiery ritual.

March/April

- **Le Pince d'Or Crab Festival:** Grand Rivière is THE spot for foodies with its fresh crab and delicious local dishes.

- **Easter (March 31):** One of the most important Christian festivals, Easter is a time of reflection and celebration. Good Friday marks the crucifixion of Christ, while Easter Sunday celebrates his resurrection.

- **Martinique Fair Expo (April 17):** Dive into the island's culture and economy at this lively five-day event with tons of products and services on display.

May

- **Labor Day (May 1):** A day to rest and honor all the hard workers on the island.

- **Tchimbe Raid (May 11-12):** Hiking enthusiasts, this one's for you! Explore Martinique's incredible landscapes during this longstanding event.

- **Slavery Abolition Day (May 22):** Martinique remembers its fight for freedom with tributes and reflection.

- **Sainte-Marie Culinary Week:** Get your taste buds ready – this is all about celebrating Martinique's unique flavours!

June

- **La Fête de la Musique:** Music fills the streets – zouk, reggae, calypso – there's something for everyone during this vibrant festival.

- **Madiflora Flower Fair:** Orchids, tropical blooms... prepare to be dazzled by the island's floral beauty.

July

- **Fort-de-France Cultural Festival (All July):** Celebrate Martinique and Caribbean culture with music, art, and events throughout the city.

- **National Holiday (July 14):** Parades, fireworks, and a celebration of all things French – Martinique knows how to party!

- **Le Tour de Martinique:** Like a smaller Tour de France, cyclists' race through the island's stunning landscapes.

- **Banana Festival:** Celebrate Martinique's favorite fruit with unique food creations and tons of fun at the Musee de la Banane de l'Habitation Limbé.

- **Mercury Beach (Late July):** Get ready for the hottest beach party in the Caribbean! Music, crowds, and fun in the sun.

August

- **Assumption Day (August 15):** A quiet day of reflection and spiritual observance.

- **Horse and mullet racing (August 15):** Experience a unique tradition in Sainte-Marie, honoring the Virgin Mary with exciting races.
- **Baccha Festival (August 17-18):** Get ready for a huge music festival at Pointe Faula – it's one of the most popular summer events!
- **Tour des Yoles Rondes:** Think Carnival on the water! These traditional yawl boat races are exciting to watch.
- **Biguine Jazz Festival:** Music lovers unite! Enjoy the blend of traditional sounds and jazzy rhythms.

September

- **Heritage Days:** Explore historic buildings and monuments usually closed to the public – it's a history buff's dream!

- **Semaine de la Gastronomie (Gastronomy Week):** Celebrate French cuisine and Martinique's unique flavors with special events and delicious experiences.

November

- **Armistice Day (November 11):** Martinique honors those who've sacrificed for peace.

- **La Belle Martinique:** Cyclists of all levels get a scenic tour of the island's most beautiful spots.

- **Raid des Alizés (November or December):** This women-only sporting adventure celebrates strength and Martinique's stunning landscapes.

- **Sainte-Cécile: musicians' festival** (November 22): Get ready for free concerts and a celebration of music all across the island.

- **Martinique International Half Marathon (Late November):** Runners from around the world test their endurance in this long-standing event.

December

- **Martinique Jazz Festival:** Get ready for soulful jazz from local and international artists.

- **Rum Festival:** Experience the island's rum heritage and delicious food at the St. James Distillery.

- **TransMartinique (December 7-8):** Hiking enthusiasts, this is the ultimate challenge! Explore Martinique's incredible trails during this multi-day event.

- **Chanté Nwel:** Traditional Christmas carols fill the air! Holiday markets and festivities make this a magical time.

- **The "Boucans de la Baie" (December 30):** End the year with a bang! Fort-de-France puts on a spectacular firework display over the bay.

- **New Year's Eve:** Fort-de-France explodes with color! Fireworks, parties, and pure joy as the island celebrates a fresh start.

Maps

Martinique

SCAN CODE TO VIEW THE INTERACTIVE MAPS WITH RECOMMENDATIONS

Fort de France

SCAN CODE TO VIEW THE INTERACTIVE MAPS WITH RECOMMENDATIONS

Sainte Anne

SCAN CODE TO VIEW THE INTERACTIVE MAPS WITH RECOMMENDATIONS

Sainte Pierre

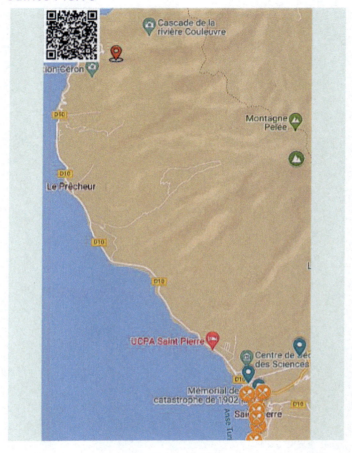

SCAN CODE TO VIEW THE INTERACTIVE MAPS WITH RECOMMENDATIONS.

Trois Ilet

SCAN CODE TO VIEW THE INTERACTIVE MAPS WITH RECOMMENDATIONS.

Le Francois

SCAN CODE TO VIEW THE INTERACTIVE MAPS WITH RECOMMENDATIONS.

Le Diamant

SCAN CODE TO VIEW THE INTERACTIVE MAPS WITH RECOMMENDATIONS.

You could also explore other books by the author....

Printed in Great Britain
by Amazon